HARRY'S
LAST
STAND

12/2018

Dear Dan,
This guy had
something to say
right to the end.
Thought you might
enjoy hearing from
someone of Papa's generation.
Glad you are my love
brother Cin

HARRY'S LAST STAND

HOW THE WORLD MY GENERATION BUILT IS FALLING DOWN, AND WHAT WE CAN DO TO SAVE IT

HARRY LESLIE SMITH

ICON

First published in the UK and USA in 2014 by
Icon Books Ltd, Omnibus Business Centre,
39–41 North Road, London N7 9DP
email: info@iconbooks.com
www.iconbooks.com

This edition published in the UK and USA in 2014 by Icon Books Ltd

Sold in the UK, Europe and Asia
by Faber & Faber Ltd, Bloomsbury House,
74–77 Great Russell Street,
London WC1B 3DA or their agents

Distributed in the UK, Europe and Asia
by TBS Ltd, TBS Distribution Centre, Colchester Road,
Frating Green, Colchester CO7 7DW

Distributed in Australia and New Zealand
by Allen & Unwin Pty Ltd,
PO Box 8500, 83 Alexander Street,
Crows Nest, NSW 2065

Distributed in South Africa by Jonathan Ball,
Office B4, The District, 41 Sir Lowry Road,
Woodstock 7925

Distributed in Canada
by Publishers Group Canada,
76 Stafford Street, Unit 300
Toronto, Ontario M6J 2S1

Distributed to the trade in the USA
by Consortium Book Sales and Distribution
The Keg House, 34 Thirteenth Avenue NE, Suite 101,
Minneapolis, MN 55413-1007

ISBN: 978-184831-736-9

Typeset in MT Bell by Marie Doherty

Printed and bound in the UK by
Clays Ltd, St Ives plc

To my Mum and Dad
Albert and Lillian
Who lived and tried to love in a time of austerity

ABOUT THE AUTHOR

Harry Leslie Smith is a survivor of the Great Depression, a Second World War RAF veteran and, at 91, an activist for the poor and for the preservation of social democracy. He has authored numerous books about Britain during the Great Depression, the Second World War and post-war austerity. He lives outside Toronto, Canada and in Yorkshire.

Contents

Prologue   xi

A Day in the Life   1

Live to Work   25

Everything Old is New Again   77

The Green and Pleasant Land   139

Eventide   167

Acknowledgements   201

I said: What is past shall be no more, shall be no more! ...
But lo! They have started to stir again ...

—Alexander Pushkin

Prologue

I remember how peace smelled on that day in May 1945. Of lilac, petrol and the rotting flesh of the dead German civilians entombed beneath the fire-bombed city of Hamburg. I was 22 years old. After four years of fighting with the RAF, I had survived and been given the chance to grow old and die in my bed. It was a day to weep for those that had been lost but also to dance and celebrate life, to drink to our good fortune.

There has not been a day in the last 60 years when I have not thought of how lucky I was. However, as I have grown older, I am no longer certain that the sacrifice my generation paid with their blood was worth the cost. Back then the people of Britain stood strong, unwilling to surrender to the tyranny of fascism, despite unimaginable civilian casualties and privations caused by the bombing that laid waste to our cities and industries. Our armed forces, comprised of boys from every compass point on our island, knew that their lives might be wagered and their futures extinguished so that our nation, our way of life, might endure. Young lads became men in the desperate clash between civilisation and barbarism.

After six years of total war, millions of casualties, millions of dead, millions of maimed lives, Britain and her allies were victorious against the scourge of Nazism. But that is not the end of the story. My generation's resolve to create a more equal Britain – a more liberal world for our children to grow up in, where merit mattered and the class system was history – was set on the battlefields of Europe.

In November, when our nation remembers her fallen soldiers and honours the lost youth of my generation, the Prime Minister, government leaders and the hollow men of business affix paper poppies to their lapels and afford the dead of war two minutes' silence. Afterwards, they speak golden platitudes about the struggle and the heroism of that time. Yet the words they speak are meaningless because they have surrendered the values my generation built after the horrors of the Second World War.

We fought in tank battles in the Sahara. We defended the skies over Britain in dogfights with the Luftwaffe. Our navy engaged in a life-or-death conflict in the battle of the north Atlantic to preserve our dominion over the seas. We were compelled to invade the armed fortress of Europe on the beaches of Normandy. In desperate battle we fought the Germans from village to town through spring and summer in our bid to liberate France. As autumn turned to winter our armies, along with those of our allies, formed a united front that pushed through the lowlands of Belgium and Holland. Those final months of conflict were intense, brutal and bloody but we buggered on until we were in the heart of Germany and on the road to Berlin and victory.

When we accepted rationing and the lack of decent housing during the post-war period of reconstruction, it was because after the bloodshed we were all focussed on building something better for everyone. And for a while it seemed that the enthusiasm that blossomed in Britain, America, France and Canada for the creation of thriving societies for the poor, the working classes, the middle classes and the wealthy would endure. It seemed genuinely possible to create nations that combined social justice with economic mobility for every citizen.

But it didn't last. By the 1970s the British economy, as well as its society, was under serious threat from inflation, weak Labour governments that weren't able to stabilise the nation's finances or control the chaos and misery that average citizens endured from an endless array of industrial strikes. In that tumultuous decade it felt like the United Kingdom had lost the plot and overreached itself in its desire to build a just society through financial stability and fair play to both worker and employer. Picket lines formed like flash mobs out of nowhere and for no apparent reason. At any given moment lorry drivers, coal miners, grave diggers or refuse collectors were on the streets demanding wage settlements that were meant to offset the horrendous cost-of-living crisis caused by inflation. However, for those who were not protected by a union it smacked of an 'I'm all right, Jack' attitude.

The 1970s were a tumultuous decade for the world's economies, but the rot really started to seep into Western democratic nations in the 80s, after the oil crisis and years of hyperinflation and chronic labour unrest. To my mind, the edifice of our civilised states started to crumble the day Ronald Reagan talked about the shining city on the hill that could be built without taxes, and when Margaret Thatcher said that come what may she would not be turned, no matter how many tears were spilled in her destruction of those who protected workers' rights. Those that had never experienced it began to talk about a golden age when taxes were low and opportunities were always available for hard workers, while the lazy perished in their own sloth.

In two short generations the tides of corporatism without conscience began to roll in and washed away the blood, sweat and tears of a hundred years of industrial workers' rights. Now, a nation that once had the courage to refigure society, to create the NHS and the modern welfare state, elects governments that are in lock-step with big business whose overriding pursuit is profit for the few at the expense of the many. We have gone from a nation that defied Hitler while the rest of Europe lay subjugated under his boot to a country that is timorous around tycoons and their untaxed offshore wealth.

These technocrats and human resource experts have reversed my generation's struggle to close the gap between the richest and the poorest. They have betrayed our dream of an equitable society with medical care, housing and education for all. They have allowed it to be taken to pieces and sold off to the lowest bidder, and broken their pledge to protect democracy and the freedoms due to every citizen in this country. This cannot be allowed to happen in respectful silence. Too many good people died. Too many sacrificed their lives for ideals that have been too quickly forgotten.

Austerity, along with the politics of fear, is being used in this country like an economic martial law. It has kept ordinary citizens in line because they are fearful of losing their jobs, being unable to make their rent, their credit card or mortgage payments.

In recent times, our governments and the right-wing media have toyed with our nervousness over the economy, over the state of the world and over our personal lives like they are poking a fire. They have sold fear to the people like the markets sell fish on Friday. We are mesmerised by this fear, stoked in a cauldron of sensationalist tabloid headlines about immigration, welfare cheats, sex scandals and militant terrorism out to extirpate Western civilisation. This perpetual war on crime, drugs, terror, immigration and benefits cheats has turned us into a society that distrusts the unknown, the weak, and the poor, rather than embracing our diversity. We have become hyper-vigilant about imaginary risks to our person and our society, but indifferent to the threats that austerity creates to our neighbourhoods, our schools, our hospitals and our friends.

Sadly, the politics of fear work. People have grown indifferent to the concerns of those who are less well off than them. It is only natural because, after all, it's a hard scrabble life for the vast majority of people in Britain these days. We have become so consumed by our personal shifting economic fortunes that we can hardly be expected to think about anyone else's. We worry, we fret; we fear for our own health and our children's safety and future. We are now always in a panic about our jobs, about our inevitable redundancy at work. We are stressed by the health of our parents and whether they can make do on their pension pot. We worry if we can save enough to be free of work for a few years before death takes us. Ultimately, we are afraid that we will be like the people from my world in the 1930s. We don't want to be like our ancestors: never able to rest, always working until we are no good for anyone and then left to die alone in some darkened corner of this island.

The middle classes are so afraid that they will become as dispossessed as the poor that they have allowed the government to use austerity as a weapon against them and their comfortable way of life. But hospital closures, bad roads and stagnant wages, along with stern cutbacks to the social welfare system affect us all – not just the indigent. I have been through this all before, and I don't want future generations to suffer as we did.

My generation never forgot the cruelty of the Great Depression or the savagery of the Second World War. We promised ourselves and our children that no one in this country would ever again succumb to hunger. We pledged that no child would be left behind because of poverty. We affirmed that education, decent housing and proper wages were a right that all our citizens deserved, no matter their class.

Throughout the years, my generation was vigilant in keeping our word to the younger generation to ensure that they did not encounter want during their lives. As a society, we fought for equal pay for equal work; unions struck for better working conditions; many organisations endeavoured to end systemic and institutional racism, while others fought against the poll tax. However, my generation grew weak through age and our resolve declined. We gradually stopped our defence against those who sought to puncture the umbrella of the social welfare state.

I suppose we had hoped that our children would keep the torch of civilisation burning while we moved into our senior years. But something happened and their resolve wasn't as strong as ours. Perhaps they got caught up in the heady world of consumerism and thought that happiness could be bought at a shop or found on an all-inclusive trip to the Bahamas, or perhaps they simply felt impotent in the face of such hardship. Whatever the reasons, from the 1980s onwards, the right-wing and New Labour governments nudged us to believe that the state was too big and needed the Midas touch of business to get it running right. Council estates were sold off, railways privatised, water put into the hand of big business. Slowly and surely, Britain and the West became societies that repudiated co-operation and socialism for corporate endeavours.

Now we live in an era when it is difficult to protect the advances made to society through our welfare state. The social safety net has been sheared by privatisation and policy makers who oppose the justice it delivers to all citizens. There are too many corporations who rely on zero-hour contracts to make enormous profits that are invested in offshore tax havens. We are losing the battle against poverty because governments and businesses won't address the disparity of wealth between those at the top of society and those who exist in the heap. Unless hunger, prejudice and rampant poverty are curtailed this nation will lose a generation, like it did mine.

When I talk to you about my past, I do so not through some golden-tinged nostalgia, or, like Monty Python's famous Yorkshiremen, in some spirit of competitive suffering, but because until you know what led to the creation of these aspects of our society, which are now so lightly discarded, you cannot understand why they were necessary.

Until you have lived through a world without a social safety net, you cannot understand what the world our leaders will leave as their legacy will be like. You cannot feel it in your marrow.

I am not a politician or an economist. I don't have a degree in PPE from Oxbridge – and I'm sure those who do will be able to pick holes in what I say. But I have lived through nearly a hundred years of history. I have felt the sting of poverty, as well as the sweetness of security and success, and I don't want to see everything we've worked for fall apart. As one of the last remaining survivors of the Great Depression and the Second World War, I will not go gently into that good night. I want to tell you what the world looks like through my eyes, so that you can help to change it.

A Day in the Life

I. First light

I woke earlier than usual this morning. My eyes opened as the sun clambered over the horizon. I lazed for a while underneath the covers, longing for the warmth of my wife, Friede, beside me, her voice whispering in my ear. I turned my body towards the wall and stared at her picture on my bedside table, a holiday pose taken a long time ago. She has been dead for more than a decade.

Getting dressed I wonder how long I have left. How many turns of this earth will be granted to me before I am just a photo on someone else's mantelpiece? Perhaps it's maudlin to dwell so much on death before breakfast, but it cannot be helped when one is 91. Death will soon come and like a publican ring his bell for last orders. At best, I have a matter of years and at worst a fluttering of months before I am dead. What is certain is that I will be gone sooner than most of you, like smoke rising up from an extinguished candle. As a son, a brother, a lover, a husband, a father and a friend I will be no more.

There will be no hymns sung on the day of my funeral. My will stipulates that there be no religious service. I have seen too much of man's wickedness to believe that this world was divinely created. And, if I am wrong, as I have been on so many other matters, I am sure that God can find it in himself to forgive me my trespasses. But there will be a wake. I have left provisions to stand my round so that those who held me close can raise a glass of beer or whiskey to my name. Later on, when the sun is high and warm, my ashes – along with those of my long-dead wife and deceased middle son – will be scattered in some serene part of Yorkshire, where I was born.

Though I am not an historian, I am history. I look back and wonder how it was possible for me to have survived the turmoil that I did. How did I make it all the way from newborn to pensioner? I don't know. Perhaps it was luck or guile, or maybe it was a combination of the two. Yet, somehow I managed to survive the Great Depression, the Second World War, Britain's post-war austerity, the upheaval of the 1960s and 70s, the threat of nuclear terror during the Cold War and this perpetual, self-renewing, self-fulfilling war on terror.

Since my birth three kings and one queen have reigned over Britain, while 21 prime ministers have ruled. During the span of my life, humanity has stumbled through revolutions, wars, economic booms and economic busts. I have seen the great and infamous bring wisdom and wreak havoc upon the world. Lenin, Hitler, Stalin, Mao, Churchill, FDR, de Gaulle, the Kennedys, Eisenhower, Nixon, Thatcher and Reagan have all been and gone. As a teenager, I remember watching the newsreel footage from the battlefields of the Spanish Civil War, and as a middle-aged man I listened to radio reports about the war in Vietnam. As an old man I have borne witness to man's greed and bloodlust as the wars in Iraq and Afghanistan have unfolded.

Nothing ever bloody changes, it seems, except the style of clothes we wear. I have travelled the world and experienced the wonders of new continents, ancient civilisations and societies on the verge of collapse. Yet everywhere I have been, I have remembered my grand-mother's blessing, spoken to me as a boy growing up in utter poverty in Yorkshire: 'Yer Barnsley bred and born. Nowt time, nowt brass is ever going to change that for thee lad, where ever thou may roam.'

Now, it is as if I am living two lives. That of the pre-sent day, but with all I have ever seen in the past lying just beneath it. It only takes a look, a smell or a moment on a bus and I am thrown back into the desperation of my boyhood in the Great Depression. When I drink a glass of milk it reminds me of all the mornings I trudged to school hungry and cold, waiting to fill my belly with the school's milk rations for the desperate. Watching a teenager on a scooter reminds me of the fear and ecstasy I experienced in Britain during the Second World War. On cloudless days, I sometimes think I hear the murderous drone of V1 rockets as they swarmed towards London. When it rains in springtime, I remember again how at the end of the war the world smelled of petrol fumes and fresh flowers.

When I read newspaper reports of the corruption in Afghanistan – where the CIA and our secret service both act like patrons in a strip club with an unlimited expense account, and where untold and unaccounted-for money from the public purse arrives from the UK and US and disappears into the moral vacuum that is the Karzai government – I can't help but think that it might as well be South Vietnam in the mid-70s, because it is going to end up that way when America and Britain disappear from the Great Game. When we are gone then the jackals known as the Taliban will descend from the mountains. They will enter the city gates of the ancient communities of Herat and Kabul. They will come as they always have in a shower of dust and Holy Scripture to terrorise a people whose only crime was to be born into a land that has been at eternal war since the days of Alexander the Great.

When I watch the beaming face of a British politician, telling me, telling Britain and telling the world that this island must decouple from Europe, that immigration is a grave concern; when I hear the familiar cadences of his xenophobia, I am reminded too much of another time when similar men spoke with more force and less nuance of a Britain for the British.

When there is a news story on Syria; when the video footage reveals a nation covered in blood, and a Middle East expert is interviewed and asserts with conviction that Assad is a war criminal while the rebels fighting him are a ragtag group who might be for democracy or they might be for the imposition of Sharia Law, I realise again that no one seems to know how it is all going to turn out. Somehow I suspect that whoever prevails, justice will not be top of their list. Instead, the victors will settle old scores as their fathers, grandfathers and great-grandfathers did before them. The losers will get a bullet to the back of the head and a shallow grave in an ancient olive grove. I feel the same when I look towards Eastern Europe where the Ukraine – a traditional blood land for empires since the days of Genghis Khan – is now being drawn and quartered by Russia, the EU and America. None of these powers came to the Ukraine with good intentions. It is all about natural resources, spheres of influence and the caprice of oligarchs. Lives will be lost, hopes of democracy dashed, dreams of economic security crushed because while this fight may have been started by people who wanted better lives for themselves and their children, it has now been co-opted by the rich and powerful who are simply looking to increase their bottom line at the expense of honest and ordinary folk.

When I hear of payday loan sharks, of food banks, of housing shortages, of medicine as something you pay for or go without and of a decent education as something only for a certain sort, it is not shock I feel but a sense of recognition.

Nothing ever changes.

II. Yesterday's men

I take my false teeth from their container and place them into my toothless mouth. I comb my hair with a brush that the RAF gave me during induction in 1941. Its bristles are still as strong as they were when they flattened the wavy locks of a boy of eighteen about to go to war. Yet looking at my sagging face, my white hair and my gnarled hands tells me what I already know. I am very old.

I fear death not because of what might await me on the other side. But I am nervous because I don't yet want to put my hat and coat on and walk out the door. I don't want to leave this world that I have lived in for almost a hundred years. It has given me an abundance of joy and of sorrow, and it is home.

Many of you, I am sure, consider me and those of my generation yesterday's men, relics from long ago. But we are not so different to you. I still have many of your familiar worries, from how to pass the time of day to how to pay my rent. Like everyone else, I grumble about money. I think I have too little; that my pension is shrinking while the cost of living is rising. Like you, I have some regrets. Why didn't I ever learn to swim or speak French? Why didn't I buy that computer stock? Like all of us, I worry about my children, despite the fact that they are halfway along in their own lives.

Most questions about life remain unanswered for me. I still don't know why our society favours some more than others. I am disgusted when I read about the bonuses doled out to banking executives as a reward for inflating their company's stock value, or for washing the money of drug cartels with as much care as the Pope cleans the feet of the poor. It angers me to see a UK government minister boast that he could live on a welfare allotment of £53 a week when 300,000 citizens need to use food banks.

I will never understand why the daily rags castigate the poor and label them scroungers with a vigour that should be reserved for corporations like Google, Amazon, Starbucks and Apple who have wantonly taken advantage of loopholes in the law in order to avoid paying their fair share of taxes. I believe that those giant corporate monoliths treat their customers and the nations they do business in with contempt because they believe that their existence is of greater importance than the individual, the state or the laws that govern the rest of us. When a corporation can earn billions of pounds in profits but only pay several million in taxes, they cease to be of net benefit to society. Regardless of the fact that what they are doing is technically legal, no economist, politician or account-ant can convince me that a company that hides its money offshore is anything but a buccaneer.

I have seen the smug faces of CEOs in Savile Row suits speak to gelded journalists on TV about 'transpar-ency', 'corporate governance' and 'fair play', and know it is all spin. I am sure their sense of decency extends to their family, friends and allies – but the rest of us are just con-sumers that must be tolerated. The entitled believe they can buy a dispirited populace with words about corporate responsibility, but they cut wages, withhold benefits and reward loyalty with redundancies. And our politicians shake their hands as they do it.

The priorities of the government and the priorities of the people have not been as divergent since the early years of the last century. Eighty years ago Britain was in desperate straits. The Great Depression had shrivelled economic growth and caused widespread unemployment and untold misery to the working and middle classes. During those horrific times, another coalition government implemented austerity measures that caused millions of Britons to sink into unendurable poverty. It tore the country into two different tribes: the employed and the down-and-out. It took a world war, the wilderness years of post-war reconstruction and the erection of the welfare state to get Britain working again. Twenty-five years were lost; a generation sacrificed before our country returned to equitable prosperity for all of its citizens.

I have lived through it once, and I have seen the misery it produced. And yet today Cameron's 21st-century government attacks this new recession with the same economic weapon used to battle the Great Depression in the 1930s. These men. They have the same suits, the same accents, the same smiles. Eighty years ago, cutting money for social services, housing and job creation was a grotesque failure. It didn't succeed then and it is certainly not going to succeed today. My generation wanted action from their government but were ignored. In our present government I see the same reckless disregard for the eroding middle classes and the disadvantaged, the unemployed and underemployed. If history is our guide, it will take another lost generation before the United Kingdom can walk clear from this economic malaise.

But the soundbites are always the same. Britain cannot afford to protect its society – we are too much in debt; we have been too profligate with our money. Ministers speak as if the entire working and middle class have been on the piss for the past twenty years. Sometimes I think that those in power believe that since John Major left office in 1997 this country has been on an extended bank holiday.

British politicians are not alone in their obsession with government debt, slashing budgets and eradicating most of the testaments to the social welfare state. America, our great ally in the war, is also our greatest friend when it comes to championing the new theory that austerity is good for society, like bleeding a patient. Watch any interview and a senator from some great state or another will put the blame squarely on President Obama. If the president doesn't fix the federal deficit, he whinges, hell and damnation wait for every American.

This senator is so caught up in his demagoguery that he forgets to mention, even in passing, that this present crisis – perhaps the greatest test of character to befall America since the crash of 1929 – might be the fault of a Republican government. The senator, like so many

11

other people in America and Britain, has conveniently developed amnesia of George W. Bush and Tony Blair's insistence that not one but two wars could be paid for like a flat-screen television with a payday loan. Yet this senator, along with the rest of the Republican party who clamoured for a war against Iraq in 2003 because Saddam supposedly had weapons of mass destruction pointed at our shores, has no difficulty stating that America is broke today because of the Democratic party's largesse. According to him, the country just can't afford to keep funding the lifestyle of its poorest citizens. To save the USA, according to the right-wing elites, the country's underprivileged – those that are underemployed and a pay cheque away from homelessness – must never be allowed to reach a lifeboat.

The solution is simple for the senator – just cut the oxygen to social welfare programmes. Eradicate major funding for food stamps, tighten eligibility, and strangle the programme like a chicken. This is the current Republican strategy in the House of Representatives, where they are trying to remove 2 million men, women and children from being eligible to receive state-funded food assistance. The Republicans think that the poor of today should rummage through restaurant and grocery store rubbish bins if they are hungry, much like my own family was forced to do in Bradford in the 1930s when there was no social safety net.

Democrat or Republican? It doesn't really matter,

because those that hold the greatest power in American politics seem to feel that America's decline is caused by the overreaching aspiration of the poor, the unemployed, the blue-collar workers, the unskilled and the ocean of undocumented illegal immigrants. The majority of decision-makers don't see that the problem with America is not its average citizen but the proverbial cream at the top, whose corporate donors and hired lobbyists perpetuate a society where the minority are granted outrageous entitlements and the cost is borne by a disenfranchised middle class.

The free world used to say that the US was the birthplace of modern democracy and innovation. Not any more. I am terrified by the wind that guides America's ship of state because she is sailing further and further into a blustering storm of jingoism. Many once espoused America to be the greatest nation on earth, but she is now as ambitious and forward-thinking as the Ottoman Empire in 1917. Today, America is a nation more at ease with stripping away the ancient rights of its citizens and workers rather than protecting them. Twenty-four US states have now enacted right-to-work legislation that dilutes the power of unions to negotiate for its members. Moreover, several states and many cities have enacted bills to remove the collective bargaining rights of workers.

Irritated, I tell myself that it's not the ordinary citizen who did these things to Britain, Europe and America. It is not the union worker, the school teacher, the IT professional in London, the plumber in Leeds or the man on disability benefits in Cheltenham who brought Britain and the West to the brink of financial ruin. It is, I say, those that rule us, and those who are the friends of our rulers, that have done this. To blame anyone else but the government, its advisors, the banks, the hedge fund managers and the corporate elite for our financial crisis is like blaming the stokers on the Titanic for hitting the iceberg.

III. Old news

As long as I can remember, I have started my morning by reading the newspaper, listening to the news on the wireless or watching the morning television news. Over the decades the technology has changed but the content remains consistent – there are still wars, famines, men murdering their wives, women murdering their boyfriends; innocent children are still brutally abused. As for politics and its reporting, governments are still trying to control what information is delivered to their citizens through the mainstream media and now also through social media platforms.

During the Second World War, the citizens of Britain understood that we were in a clash of civilisations. We accepted that the news was censored for our own good. We took it as a given that there were certain truths that we must not know. We traded some of our individual liberties for the greater good of the nation. We loaned, so to speak, our grain of salt to the government, but it was understood by everyone to be only for the war's duration.

Today, however, I don't believe that this bargain – this surrender of individual liberties between the people and the so-called powers that be – has been consentingly struck. The state has taken more and more of our legal rights, as individuals or as workers, because we didn't stop and say: 'Now just hold on a minute, Prime Minister. Where are these threats of terror, where *is* this great enemy?'

In today's complex world, the average citizen should be just as concerned about how information regarding their country's economy, government and society is relayed to them as they are about the safety of the food they ingest. Considering that the news we consume on television, radio, print or online is largely delivered to us by a handful of powerful corporations that filter, censor and sculpt the events of the day to meet their corporate or ideological view, our daily allotment of news should come, like a packet of crisps, with a list of the ingredients used to produce that editorial about the NHS, that television show about benefits scroungers or that magazine piece about Prince Charles' love of homeopathy.

During my lifetime I have watched as the technology has advanced and the concentration of economic power has become more centralised and less democratic. In the United States six gargantuan companies disseminate 90 per cent of the news that is consumed by the American public. Historically there have been only two incidences when both the repository of news and its delivery was more controlled and crafted. The first was in the medieval world, before the printing press was invented. During that time, the Roman Catholic Church believed they owned the truth, and this dogma about how to live, how to obey the laws of man and how to view the world was imparted through the church pulpit.

Almost 500 years would pass before another empire was able to craft a similar monolithic message to their laity. During Stalin's reign over the Soviet Union, he rewrote and revised the history of the Russian Revolution to conform to his ideology. Soviet newsreaders, newspapers, university lecturers and ordinary teachers were compelled to interpret the news, economic statistics and cultural events from a Stalinist perspective, or face exile to a gulag or summary execution. I'm sure you'll agree that neither are examples we should aim to emulate.

Here in Britain, we have not yet fallen so far down that rabbit hole that either corporate interest or the state absolutely controls the delivery of our news information. However, we are at a dangerous crossroads, because as in America, our country's media is owned by a few wealthy corporations and rich families. Despite the phone hacking scandals and the allegations of interfering in politics, Rupert Murdoch's News International controls an estimated 37 per cent of this country's media outlets. As for the other 63 per cent, they are held like medieval fiefdoms by men like the Russian oligarch Alexander Lebedev and business trusts like the Trinity Mirror, the Daily Mail and General Trust, and the Richard Desmond Trust.

So much power and so much control over the flow of information, news and opinion held by so few individuals can only weaken democracy. The Leveson Inquiry aptly demonstrated how these media giants have contorted the truth and ethics in their pursuit of profits over accurate and impartial reporting. Yet two years after this report was tabled, the press has still not brought its dogs to heel when it comes to attacking and vilifying those who cannot defend themselves. All one has to do is look at recent headlines in certain right-wing tabloids which pillory the poor and excoriate the left with the viciousness of a schoolyard bully. I admit this is nothing new; I experienced this form of class hatred when I was in my youth. Then, as today, these tabloids appealed to the lowest common denominator by demonising the poor, the new immigrants and the vulnerable as public enemy number one when it came to Britain's financial woes. It would be laughable if it were not so prevalent, but tabloid misinformation is as bad for our society as state-controlled *Pravda* was for communist Russia's society. When citizens are getting information which forms their opinions from tabloids that, instead of writing balanced news articles, choose to present falsehoods held together by prejudice and malicious gossip, the nation is at risk of losing its democracy. When tabloids seek to create drama, scandal and discord and the public accepts this as fact, as many of us do today, we are at the top of a very slippery slope that will lead us to a more dysfunctional and cruel society.

When I watch the news on television – and it doesn't matter which broadcaster: BBC, Sky, CNN, Fox or CBC – it all sounds tired, deflated, as if it has been written by a lobbyist or government policy maker. It seems contrived and fake, like the newsreaders are in on a joke that eludes their public. I can be in Yorkshire, Albufeira, New York or Toronto, but the message is always the same: health care is too costly, education must be about job training, immigration is too high ... It can't ever be about making a more informed citizen because culture is too costly in a world content with scripted reality television shows and blockbuster zombie movies.

Wiretaps and electronic snooping of one's personal conversations or emails are commonplace. You don't have to be an enemy of the people to be under surveillance in the USA anymore; you just have to be a member of a union or an environmental group, or simply be someone who thinks that due process under the law applies to everyone, not just Wall Street insiders.

Edward Snowden, the NSA contractor, proved this when he became a whistleblower and disclosed to the *Guardian* newspaper that our Western spy agencies are monitoring, collating, collecting and analysing everyone's emails, Facebook and twitter messages. Men like President Obama and William Hague tell us that we have nothing to fear if we have done nothing wrong, but I am not so sure. Today, they say they are looking for Islamic terrorists, but tomorrow who will the government be putting on their watch list? Environmentalists? Peace activists? Seniors concerned about their pension or the preservation of the NHS? A government's lists of potential threats to its authority gets larger as it leaves more and more of the nation's citizens disgruntled and disenfranchised.

At what point does what you give up while fighting a war mean winning it no longer matters?

IV. Desperate times

I turn the television off and prepare my coffee, my mind full of stories of poverty and privation. I heap an enormous amount of sugar into the cup and begin to stir. Each clink of my coffee spoon across the cup begins to sound more and more like the bells wrapped round the bridal of a horse. A dim memory rises up in me from long ago, one that for the better part of 80 years I have tried to bury deep inside.

It is the melancholy sound of horse's hooves making a steady beat on ancient cobblestone streets. It is a noise and image from my days as a child in Bradford, where we moved after my dad lost his job as a miner in Barnsley. I see this poor creature as if I am right there at this very moment, standing before them on the side of a street. I watch this worn dray horse pulling a rag-and-bone man's wagon filled with rubbish and items scavenged from the tips of the well-to-do. I see a man holding the reins who wears a worker's cap while a fag end clings to his lower lip. Beside him is a beggar boy – not his son, not his assistant, but me – who the carriage driver has taken pity on.

'Come on lad, hop aboard. If you help with my rounds, I'm sure I can find some broken boxes of cereal in the back of the cart. You can take them home to your mam and dad.'

This is a poverty that does not exist in living memory for most people in the UK, and certainly not for the millionaires who populate our government and brand the poor as scroungers. When the Great Depression struck I was six, and by the time I was seven my family was penniless, living rough in a doss house – cheap, spartan one-room squats where society's unfortunates ate, slept and fretted about whether they could afford to pay the weekly rent.

It was a desperate time for everyone and it called for desperate measures. Lives and futures were sacrificed for a scrap of bread or a slice of mutton. My childhood ended in the first year of school, and I became an adult at seven. The man who drove the rag-and-bone cart was just one of many who I begged from to keep my parents fed until I was able to find work as a beer barrow boy. The harsh visions from my boyhood and the poverty I endured have haunted me throughout my adult life and followed me well into my old age, and in my dotage I still feel my chest tighten when I see a homeless lad outside a tube station.

When I was 22 I was in the RAF, and the war against Hitler was near its end. My unit at the time was moving through Holland towards Germany. As I rode in an open-backed lorry, I witnessed the true horror of Nazism. At the side of the road, between abandoned and gutted vehicles, stood a multitude of young children. Each one was emaciated, hollowed out by years of privation. Many had been reduced to eating tulip bulbs in order to survive. They were starving, and in their hungry eyes I recognised the famine of my boyhood. Naturally we were outraged at the cruelty of the Nazis. We stopped our convoy and did our best to make sure those children were provided with adequate food rations before moving on to Germany. The portrait of those innocent children, caught up in a vicious war, enraged me and I wanted to damn the whole German race for this evil – that is, until I began to encounter endless rivers of German children who looked just as famished as their Dutch counterparts. I started to see ordinary Germans as victims of this war just as much as we were. It buttressed my innate belief that all of us, every man, woman and child in the world, is just one turn of the card, one spin of the roulette wheel away from ruin and suffering.

Today, after the newspaper and the newsreaders' reports about cuts to the NHS, austerity measures for the welfare system, corruption in Afghanistan and bloodshed in Syria, the memories from my past become particularly strong. I feel as if I am still a little boy scrounging for sustenance in the Great Depression. Back then I was afraid, angry, hungry, humiliated by my family's fall into the gutter. Thinking about it now makes my hands tremble and brings tears to my eyes. I am too old to be forced to remember this, too frail to plunge through the weeds and murky depths of my boyhood. It hurts too much, but then I stop and I grow enraged. I think to myself that my past should have just been that. It should have been a footnote in a story about a long-ago time, best forgotten. Stories about my past should end with: 'Well, Granddad, that was in your day. Thank God we've got it all sorted now.'

'Cobblers,' I mutter to myself. It's all cobblers. Nothing has been sorted, nothing was fixed. I know this because UNICEF has just issued a report that states that by the year 2020 one in four British children will live in poverty. How is it possible, I wonder, that in 21st-century Britain, so many people can go without proper food, adequate shelter, medical care? The revelation stings because I know that those children who are born into poverty today are as unlucky as I was, born in 1923. They are destined to be crushed and defeated with the same ferocity as my generation was eight decades ago – unless we all put a stop to it.

The weak and vulnerable today may have more creature comforts than my generation, it's true, but we share the same emptiness, the same despair caused by politicians who promise that change is coming, like a mighty wind. But it is only bluster because nothing ever blows down towards the down-and-out in Britain or in America. When I watched footage of the riots in Britain in 2011, or of the Occupy protests around the world, I recognised that same urgency, that same anger that my parents' generation felt. So many children, adults and even pensioners live on the kerbside of desperation. Yet the press, the government and too many ordinary people ignore it. They prefer to be like the citizens of Pompeii, and look away from the smoking volcano.

Live to Work

I. Health care

What is it that people say – 'at least you've got your health'?

Because so much of what I experienced in a world before the welfare state, before the rise in workers' rights, is so alien to most of you, I want to try and describe what it was like back then for normal people just trying to live: do a fair day's toil, feed their family; and what happened when your health failed and you could no longer work.

A midwife with a penchant for gin delivered me into the arms of my exhausted mother on a cold, blustery day in February 1923. I slept that night in my new crib, a dresser drawer beside her bed, unaware of the troubles that surrounded me. Because my dad was a coal miner, we lived rough and ready in the hard scrabble Yorkshire town of Barnsley. Money and happiness didn't come easily for the likes of us.

Considering the hunger, the turmoil and the squalor in Britain during the early years of the 20th century, it was miraculous that I lived to see my third birthday. That I survived colic, flu, infection, scrapes and bangs without the benefits of modern sanitation, hygiene or health care, I must give thanks to my sturdy peasant genes. As a baby, I was ignorant of the great sorrow that enveloped England and Europe like a damp, grey fog. The nation was still in mourning for her dead from the world's first Great War. It had ended only five short years before my arrival. Nearly a million British soldiers had been killed in that conflict. It had begun in farce in 1914 and ended in bloody tragedy in 1918. In four years that war killed over 37 million men, women and children around the world.

Even when the guns across the battlefields were made dumb by peace, the killing didn't stop. Death refused to take a holiday and a pestilence stormed across the globe. It was called the Spanish Flu. The pandemic lasted until 1921 and it erased 100 million people from the ledger book of the living.

While I sucked on my mother's teat through the first weeks and months of my life, and learned to recognise my mum's face, her smell, her touch and her voice, the world outside of my tiny grasp descended into madness. Lenin and his communists controlled Russia and had unleashed a bloody terror against capitalists, aristocrats and anyone who they thought posed a threat to the new Soviet order. Mussolini ruled Italy with a new ideology called fascism. Hungary and Austria struggled through inflationary chaos, while Germany imploded into the anarchy that provided a perfect breeding ground for Nazism.

The world was in crisis, and in the coffee houses and bars across Europe trade unionists, social democrats, lawyers, teachers and common men and women argued and debated. The question was always the same: how could we free mankind from the tyranny of war and the slavery of poverty? The answers, however, were divergent. Some wanted revolution and to topple governments, others argued that the current status quo was best because capitalism seemed to fit man's need to control his environment. Others still championed social democracy and said that perhaps socialism was the sanest route to govern a nation's economy and society.

In my own village, the talk was just as radical but slightly more practical. Down at their locals, men like my father, my grandfather and my uncles talked to one another about the affairs of the day. Between discussions about football and test matches, they would find time to speak about how their labour for the pit owners was undervalued. Many believed, like my dad, that a worker should be paid a fair day's wages for a fair day's work.

Much later on, I learned the reason why my family, like millions of other honest working families, was so sorely abused by the caprice of economics. It wasn't because we were unlucky, lazy or intellectually deficient, as we were led to believe by those who governed us, instructed us, employed us or provided us with religious comfort. No, it was far more sinister and cynical than even the 19th-century philosopher Malthus' dictum that 'to prevent the recurrence of misery is beyond the powers of Man'. The problem was that our nation was stratified and defined by an exacting social class caste system. It was a perfectly constructed pyramid that was built upon one premise: that the multitudes were not equal to the few who ruled them. Since the masses were deemed inferior by those who stood above them economically, it was not considered appropriate that we share in the wealth of this nation.

On this hierarchy of humanity, my family stood at the lowest rung – the working poor of the working class. We were the human capital that drove the nation's economy. We were the brute strength that dug coal, spun wool on looms into cloth, worked in service to tend to the needs of the well-to-do, built ships and roads or erected the skylines that were beginning to take shape in our great cities.

Our contribution to society was treated largely with contempt by those who considered themselves our betters. As there were so many of us, the upper classes thought of us as a good farmer thinks of his livestock. We were an investment that should be fed and housed and nothing more. It was for that reason that my tribe – the ordinary, humble worker – lived in slums or in crudely constructed tenements that were no better than stalls for horses.

Like most people in Barnsley, my family occupied a terraced house. It was built back-to-back and in a row of ten units. There was little space, privacy or comfort for us or any of the other occupants. It was just a place to rest your head after spending ten hours hacking coal from the side of a rock face hundreds of feet below ground. Three walls out of four were connected on to another household. The floors were made of hard slate rock and were sparsely covered with old rags that had been hand-woven into coarse mats. The interior walls were comprised of wet limestone that was covered in a gruel-thin whitewash that never seemed to look clean.

Slums, like the ones I resided in as a boy, remained a blight upon the British landscape until the post-war Labour government began to sort out our 20th-century housing crisis. It was a herculean task because the Attlee government had to rectify the damage done to housing stock by Hitler's bombs, and also eradicate the hovels where most of the working class subsisted while toiling away in low-wage industrial jobs in the country's factories, mills, foundries and mines. It was an arduous process, and it took decades for our nation to replace the slums of my youth with decent housing estates, where families were able to raise their children with pride.

Today, however, we face a housing challenge that is just as great as the one my generation faced in the 1940s and 50s. Now, we must be as enlightened and as far-sighted as those men who led the government after the war was won against the Nazis. It is essential that we institute revolutionary and bold initiatives to provide affordable housing for all our citizens.

Where and how we live is as important to the nation's well-being as health care, education and decent paying jobs. As a society we shouldn't accept that housing initiatives be left solely in the hands of the private sector, who have created a fragile bubble through myopia and greed. Naturally, investors may grumble about what happens to their returns if the state develops a coherent national action plan to house the country's citizens. But in the end if we listen to the stridency of the city hedge fund managers and accept that speculation is the right way to construct a housing strategy, homelessness will become a pandemic that will infect not just poor but the middle class as well.

We must develop a plan to provide affordable and decent housing for the 21st century, because what we have now is only benefiting the speculators. The housing crisis is so acute that in London buying a home is a dream that few young people will realise. The cost of having a place to kip has become so prohibitive that one in ten renters in London is on a waiting list for affordable housing.

As for those individuals who rent flats or homes across the country, many of them pay more than 35 per cent of their gross income to have a roof above their heads. For low-income workers the housing situation is even worse because one third of rental properties are out of their economic reach. The over-inflated cost of housing coupled with the working poor and the young being priced out of the housing market is a recipe for civil disorder, as much as inflated food prices were during the 19th and early 20th century for the revolutions that flared up in France, Germany and Russia. If the government doesn't get a grip on this crisis, the younger generation will naturally lose faith in our current political and economic process. At this juncture in history, our society must progress and fix the deficits in our housing policy or we are doomed to repeat the misery experienced by me and so many of my generation.

As a country, do we really want to go all the way back to that unjust world of my youth, where might was right? It terrifies me because I remember what it was like to live in those houses that weren't fit to kennel a dog. When I was still a lad in Barnsley, I remember that in summer our home was hot, in autumn damp, and in winter bitterly cold, while spring was as wet as autumn again. Ours was no different from any terraced squat in the country. Each one of them was a dank, grubby little warren that left one claustrophobic. We had a scullery, a cramped parlour and two rooms upstairs that were used for sleeping. The house had no electricity and only the parlour and scullery possessed a gas light fixture. After sunset, it sputtered and hissed a gloomy yellow light that illuminated our poverty. I shared a room with my older sister, Alberta. We slept together on a straw mattress that was host to many insects and reeked of time and other people's piss. Its covering was made from a rough material that was as uncomfortable to me as the occasions when my father tickled my face with his moustache. Depending on the season, I slept in my undershirt or remained fully clothed. During the cold months, Alberta and I nestled together and shared our body heat to stave off the chilling frost beating against the windowpane. Our parlour had no furniture except a stool and an upright piano that had come as part of my dad's legacy from his father. But it stood mute against the wall because the room was occupied by my infirm and dying eldest sister, Marion.

At the age of four she had contracted tuberculosis, which was a common disease among our class. Her ailment was caused because my parents were compelled to live in a disease-ridden mining slum at the end of the Great War. Eventually my parents were able to leave the slum but by then the damage had already been done to my sister's health, and the TB spread into her spine. It left her a deformed paraplegic with a hunchback. For the last twelve months of her life, Marion was totally dependent on my mother to be fed, bathed and clothed. In those days, there was no national health service; one either had the dosh to pay for your medicine or you did without. Your only hope for some medical care was the council poor house that accepted indigent patients.

As a young lad, I was encouraged by my parents to spend time with my ailing sister. I think it was because they knew that she was dying and they wanted me to remember her for the rest of my life. I didn't comprehend illness or death because I was only three, so I contented myself with playing near her sick bed. On some occasions I told her nonsense stories, but my sister couldn't respond to my kindness because the disease had destroyed her vocal cords. Even though she was in extreme pain while the TB ate away at her spine and invaded her vital organs, she was silent. My sister always seemed to be looking past me with her large expressive eyes. Perhaps she was waiting for death, or perhaps she found the gas light casting shadows on the opposite wall an appealing distraction from the monotony of the pain that consumed her ten-year-old body.

TB was known in the 19th century as the poet's disease, but I saw no lyricism in the way it killed Marion. As the autumn days grew shorter in 1926, so did the time my sister had to live. Her last weeks were unbearable but she still fought death. She thrashed her arms about in defiance against the coming end to her life. My parents tried to calm her by stroking her hair or singing to her, but she wasn't pacified. Instead, Marion wept silent tears and continued to struggle with so much ferocity that in the end my dad reluctantly restrained her to her bed with a rope.

My parents decided that there was nothing more that could be done for Marion in their care, so they arranged for her to be placed in our local workhouse infirmary. It was the last stop for many people who were too poor to pay for a doctor or proper hospital care. The workhouse in our community was a forbidding building that had been constructed during the age of Dickens. In the century before I was born it was used to imprison debtors, house orphans and provide primitive health care to the indigent.

By the time Marion was sent there, it no longer was used as a prison. However, orphans, the sick and those with communicable diseases were still incarcerated behind its thick, towering black walls.

On one of the last days in September my mother pawned her best dress and my father's Sunday suit and hired a man with an old dray horse and cart to come to our house and collect Marion. When he arrived my dad carried Marion outside and carefully placed her into the delivery carriage where my mother was waiting for her.

Alberta and I stood on the side of the street and waved goodbye to Marion. I asked my dad where my sister was going and he mournfully replied: 'She's going to a better place than here.' Afterwards, he put his arms around me and Alberta and we watched the horse-drawn carriage slowly plod down our road towards the workhouse infirmary.

That was the last time I saw my sister Marion alive. She died a month later in the arms of my mother. When she died there was no wake, no funeral service and even much later there was no headstone erected to mark her brief passage in life. My family, like the rest of our community, was just too poor to afford the accoutrements of mourning. We relied on my dad's minuscule salary just to keep us with a roof over our heads and dry in the perpetual hard luck rain of Yorkshire. Even my dead sister's landau was quickly dispatched to the pawnbroker's shop where it was swapped for a few coins to help feed her hungry living siblings.

My sister's body was committed to a pauper's pit and interned in an unmarked grave along with a dozen other forgotten victims of penury. My parents didn't even have a picture to remember their daughter's life. To the outside world, it was as if she was never there, but for our family her life and her end profoundly affected us. My father never mentioned Marion's name again. It wasn't out of callousness or disrespect, but because her death festered in his soul like a wound that never healed. For the rest of his life my dad carried with him an unwarranted guilt that he was responsible for Marion's tuberculosis, and it cut him deep. As for my mother, she often talked about Marion. As my family stumbled from misery to calamity, through the pitch dark of the Great Depression, my mother invoked my dead sister's name as a warning that the workhouse awaited each of us, unless the world and our circumstances changed.

So it has always been difficult for me to listen to politicians, proud possessors of health insurance and shares in private health care companies, when they talk about how the health service that we fought so hard to build must change.

II. A long way down

While Marion had been battling for her life, there had been a different sort of battle going on around us that I was not aware of. My father had foreseen the General

Strike. He may not have had a degree in economics, but he knew that when the mine owners demanded their workers take drastic cuts in their pay to maintain their profits during a recession, life in our community was going to become unbearable.

It seemed to my father and his fellow miners that it was only fair play that they should be paid a decent and proper income for their dangerous labour. After all, each and every working day these men risked their lives by digging coal hundreds of feet below the moors of Britain. Between 1850 and 1914, 90,000 miners perished in accidents both below and above the surface. There had been measured improvements to worker safety in British mines after the Great War. Yet for every life saved many were still lost to rock slides, cave-ins, explosions or industrial mishaps. Men like my father worked by torchlight in cramped and unhealthy conditions. If they weren't killed in the mines, they generally died from cancers caused by exposure to toxic substances. Black lung, TB, heart disease and arthritis ensured that a miner's retirement years were short and painful. I keep that in mind, whenever anyone criticises the power of unions nowadays.

In my childhood the coal that the country's miners hacked out of the treacherous earth fuelled our nation's prosperity. It was only natural that miners like my dad wanted more than the thrupenny life that their current wages allotted them. By the time I was weaned and walking, I watched from the corner of my mother's apron strings those men of the pits, the looms, the shipyards, down their tools and join Britain's first General Strike. In May 1926, the country was shuttered while workers from the north and south converged upon London to demand a better deal for the millions who were at the bottom rungs of society.

In the House of Lords, the Houses of Parliament and in the capital's financial sector the General Strike was considered to be treason, an attack on the crown. The barons of steel and coal concurred and asked that strong measures be taken to bring to heel these revolutionary upstarts who didn't know their place in British society. The government agreed and feared that if the strike was to be protracted, the nation would collapse into Bolshevism. However, instead of ceding to the strikers' demands for better wages and working conditions, the government ordered the army out on to the streets and instructed the police to show no restraint against the protestors.

In two weeks the strike was over because the moneyed class and the government had used every resource at their disposal to intimidate and pressgang the workers back to their servitude. Like a defeated race enslaved by a greater power, the strikers from almost all directions of our island returned to work without having gained anything, and having lost money through lack of wages.

The miners, however, refused to yield, and instead continued their strike and chanted in defiance, 'not a penny off the pay, not a minute off the day', while the police violently attempted to break up their protest marches. For seven more months they held out against the government, the mine owners and the hired thugs sent to intimidate their families. They withstood hunger, poverty and the despair that comes from having no income. They even endured the shame of their wives begging for bread on the high streets of Yorkshire because their children were starving.

We were lucky that my father had some reserve savings from his father's inheritance. It wasn't much but it was enough to keep our stomachs full during those hungry months when the miners refused to work without just compensation, though by the end of the strike it was all gone. Without it, we would have been destitute like the rest of Britain's poor who lived from weekly pay packet to pay packet.

The day before Marion died the nation's miners called off the General Strike and agreed to return to their collieries. The strikers had failed to secure any concessions from the mine owners, but six months of pickets and protest had left them battered and financially busted. They were starving and willing to take what was given to them by a cruel profit-driven industry that had no compassion for its workers. The miners returned to work at a reduced salary. To the coal-faced men of the pits the sound of the screeching work whistle played like a funeral dirge. It beckoned them to return to the darkness of the mines and dig for the prosperity of the mine owners who lived in stately mansions.

In Britain during the first decades of the 20th century anyone who worked in heavy industry or mining was just one accident away from homelessness. If you injured yourself on the job the state wasn't going to take care of you, except to grant you a temporary bare subsistence dole. As for your employer, they had little legal obligation to provide compensation for an employee injured on the job site. Even if you belonged to a union, they had few resources to maintain an injured worker for long on their insurance rolls.

The best most workers had to keep them safe at work was a lucky talisman hung around their necks. They hoped that superstition would protect them against rockslides, cave-ins and mechanical equipment that had run amok. As for my dad, he put his faith in himself and believed that he, unlike every other miner, was invincible against exhaustion, poor work conditions and bad luck.

My dad had suffered his fair share of mishaps in the pits, but they had always been minor incidents and he believed that he would continue to be a miner until retirement. Unfortunately, it didn't work out that way for him. One day, when I was five, my dad's good fortune came to a permanent end. His accident occurred after a long, arduous shift hewing coal from the side of a rock face. He was strong man and no stranger to the toil and dangers of his occupation but he carelessly shifted an enormous boulder. The weight of the rock was too much for him and caused a hernia.

At first my dad considered the incident an inconsequential accident, but within a week the rupture made it impossible for him to work below ground. His foreman transferred him to the surface where he toiled as an ordinary labourer until he was too infirm to work and was let go. Our family was provided poor relief by the council. It was ten shillings a week. As a family of four we were expected to buy food, pay for our shelter and keep our squat warm on less than a pound a week, and soon we began to suffer the effects of starvation.

It had been hard enough for my parents to keep the bailiffs from the door on my dad's salary as a miner, but when he became a surface labourer it was near impossible for them to pay the rent. But my parents were reluctant to move to cheaper lodgings. I suspect they feared for the health and well-being of both me and my sister if we moved into a more derelict neighbourhood, given what had happened to Marion.

So we stayed in our home that Christmas and into the new year. My parents stayed out of pride, out of shame and probably out of fear of what was going to become of us on my dad's reduced wages. Yet despite the cold gloom and half-light of winter, that Christmas was as close to magical as I can remember from my childhood. We celebrated and defied our poverty, our mourning over Marion and our anxiety for the future with passion and happiness at being in each other's company.

On Christmas day, my father entertained us by playing

carols on the piano while my mother prepared a goose. Our feast had been bought at the expense of my mother's wedding ring that had been put in hawk at the pawnbroker's shop. For a present, I was given a toy train engine that my parents were never able to equal in extravagance during subsequent Christmases. In the years that followed, my sister and I would speak of that Christmas as if we had received the riches of Croesus from our parents, because it was one of the last moments that we remembered our family being truly happy.

When there was finally no hope for my dad to return to his job, we upped sticks from Barnsley to Bradford, where we thought life might be easier. Now, when I travel to Bradford it is to visit the dead. My mother, my father, my sisters, my boyhood friends; everyone I knew here has turned to dust. No one from my youth has survived into old age. For me, this place is a necropolis. I enter it and remember all those lives that were abandoned by their country, during another period of austerity.

When my family crossed through its city gates in 1929, my life in short pants was done. We had come on a midnight flit from Barnsley because my dad's poor relief had run out and we weren't able to meet our rent payments. We came to this city with nothing more than the clothes on our backs. We were refugees in a ferocious tempest of austerity. On the other side my parents had hoped to find economic security, but instead discovered shuttered factories, breadlines and grotesque urban destitution.

Innocence, hope, love, friendship, trust – those talismans of civilisation were extinguished for me and my family in the ancient shantytowns of this city.

In my innocence, I longed for the familiar squalor of Barnsley, because at least there I felt like I was part of a family, not a runt running with a pack of wild dogs. In the mining town of my birth I had experienced something akin to childhood, albeit one as short and fragile as an arctic summer.

Here in our new surroundings I didn't feel safe. Bradford was a large, carnivorous metropolis that swallowed up families not sharp enough or lucky enough to navigate its mean streets. As we made our way from the bus stop to our new squat, I held my sister's hand while my parents forged through the unfamiliar streets a few steps ahead of us. This city seemed a desolate place to me. The buildings looked filthy, and on the pavement the homeless loitered with the unemployed.

I felt afraid, so I asked my sister Alberta what our new home would be like.

'It will be a palace of right bloody wonders,' she said with a harsh laugh. 'Ain't that right, Mam?' Whereupon our mum told her to shut her gob.

When summer came during that first year of living doss house rough, I was homesick again for Barnsley. It wasn't that our lives before Bradford had been particularly pleasant, because they hadn't. But it was the only home I'd ever known, and there was a normalcy to our poverty there. Later on, after we had more or less settled into our routine of being skint in Bradford, I took a walk around our new surroundings with my father. Naively, I asked him if we could go back to visit our old neighbourhood. 'Lad, we can never go back to Barnsley. It is done for us there.'

And so it was, because the longer we were imprisoned in the malicious slums of Bradford, the more we changed as individuals and as a household. The bonds that held us together as a family were dissolved in the harsh acid bath of poverty.

Coming to the city was our only choice, outside of starving in Barnsley, but it gutted my dad. He wasn't able to find work in Bradford because the unemployment rate was horrendous and he didn't have the right connections to get a job. For him, not working was like a death sentence from a terminal illness. He felt hopeless. It ruined his confidence, his self-respect and destroyed his health. My mother was bitter and broken by her children's hungry anguish. Alberta, three years my senior, was defiant, rude and reckless in the face of our ruin. As for me, I felt vulnerable, naked and at the mercy of elements stronger than myself. The winds of poverty blew me where they liked because I was just a boy living in a world where the rules of civilised society were suspended.

Mum was sharp with her children but her rebukes to my dad were savage. She liked to set into him after he had returned from his walk to the government relief office. He'd come into our rooms in quiet defeat. My sister and I would greet him warmly but my mother froze his welcome with a contemptuous stare that transmitted both hate and hurt.

Dad would go and stand by our empty grate, his coat still wrapped around him like he was one of Napoleon's soldiers lost in Russia's cold wastes. He kept his once strong miner's back to us while mum berated him as a man, husband and father. 'You've put us into the fiery pits of hell,' my mum screamed at my father. My dad, always apologetic, always ashamed, turned towards her and pleaded: 'Don't worry lass; it's always darkest before the light. You'll see, it'll be right as rain. Work is bound to turn up for me.' His solicitations didn't soothe my mother's concerns because she knew that the days of steady but poorly paid labour were for the history books. My mum was right, because those jobs never came back for my dad or his kind. As for my parents, the love that had once joined them together was bitten down to the quick from enforced unemployment.

In the end, my mum could take it no more and she proved that although love may be thicker than water, it is has no value compared to bread and a roof over your head. When dad because of injury, no work and no social safety net could no longer provide for us, he was out on his ear. Mum looked for another man she hoped could put food on the table with more regularity than my dad. A man with a job. Eventually she took up with a pig man called Bill. As for my dad, he lived rough for a while and ultimately ended up dying in a doss, heartbroken and with only a few pennies to his name not far from where I spent my childhood. And as for us? We ended up in the lower-class neighbourhood of Boothtown Road in Halifax when Bill got a job as a butcher, and that's where I spent my teen-age years. My parents had truly loved each other but the harsh times conspired against their civilised souls. During the Great Depression, it was for my family and everyone else a fight to the finish and only the strong endured. Love does not survive both a violent financial tempest, a global economic shipwreck and then being tossed about on a cruel, violent sea.

In the 80-plus years since I was a bairn, housing and health care may have improved for the working poor, but since Thatcher's rule this country has been march-ing against the stream of progress. When the Iron Lady said that 'there is no society', I immediately understood what she wanted. She wanted 1980s Britain to resemble her childhood and mine when there was no welfare state. Considering her father's wealth and position in Grantham, it was probably the best of times for Margaret but for many of us it was the worst. Therefore, it doesn't surprise me that during her tenure Britain suffered two recessions, the beginning of the end for labour unions and unemploy-ment that matched that of the Great Depression.

When Tony Blair came to power in 1997, he said he felt our pain, like our own glib version of Bill Clinton.

However, he didn't heal the deep wounds cleaved into Britain by Thatcherism. Instead, Blair and New Labour completed her revolution by keeping taxes low for our country's wealthiest citizens, deregulating the banks and allowing much of social service delivery to be privatised. Under his watch, the gap between the richest and the poorest citizens increased.

The sorry mess Britain and America is mired in today was sown by a generation of politicians on both the left and right who ignored early 20th-century history. Whether it was done from hubris, incompetence or greed, the damage to today's society has been done and we have sacrificed another generation to economic stagnation.

When I watched George Osborne deliver the government's most recent budget, which tried to bring bread and circuses to the people but settled on beer and bingo because it was cheaper, I realised that we have regressed to a more sanitised, less deadly version of my youth. Hope now, as then, is as hard to come by as a decent paying job. The government wants the public to believe that the cause of our recession was not the gluttony of the financial sector or corporations refusing to pay their fair share of tax, but the fault of the lowly benefit seeker. This is why the government has made it harder for the newly unemployed to collect welfare. Now they will have to wait seven days before they can sign up to their job-seeker benefits. It is a punitive measure that is meant to humble the unemployed. When my father went on the dole in the 1930s, he too was made to wait for his pittance and let his children do without their tea. Governments that create this mechanism to delay benefit payments want the unemployed to feel that they are responsible for their situation. They want those who find themselves redundant to be more willing to accept jobs that pay less and provide fewer benefits.

For the unemployed these are dark, grim days, especially in the economically ravaged north. The cause is not, as some politicians have reported, that the British-born job seekers are too demanding when it comes to employment. It has nothing to do with lack of initiative or sloth; it is that the job market has become so competitive that employers are not compelled to offer living wages with decent benefits.

When the government introduced, without any oversight, workfare as an alternative to benefits they set in motion the Poundland scandal. The 'work for your benefits' scheme, where the unemployed were forced to work for free to show willing, was quite rightly deemed unlawful. The bureaucrats and government ministers that drafted our draconian anti-poverty legislation showed both heartlessness and true ignorance towards our unemployment catastrophe. This country is not made up of the fabled ant and grasshopper but of regions that are begging for work. Look north to Hull and you will see the true tragedy of unemployment. In that city there are 55 job seekers for every available position. Further south in Nottingham, 1,700 people applied for just eight jobs at

Costa Coffee. When almost 2,000 people compete for less than 20 work positions, it prods me back to the 1930s, and to those itinerate workers that my family shared space with in our doss. They too ran from one job site to next and looked for work like stray dogs beg for scraps.

The situation is truly grim for our disabled citizens, who are currently tested by ATOS, a private, profit-driven corporation. This company processes close to 20,000 eligibility claims a week and is ruthless in denying benefits to disabled citizens based upon questionable testing methods. The callipers used to assess whether someone is entitled to a disability benefit are woefully inaccurate. Last year, the DWP had to overturn and reinstate benefits to a third of ATOS's claimants who had been denied benefits. The government has recently stated that they will not be renewing this corporation's contract. However, it should be noted that the agenda to deny eligibility to benefits claimants is set by the government, not by the private corporations who execute the will of the DWP. So in all likelihood it will make little difference to those who must prove their merit to case workers whose mandate is cost savings at the expense of a well-maintained social safety net.

The disappointment of underemployment and the fear and anxiety that today's workers have for their futures cuts me deeply. It reminds me too much of the economic crises that also destroyed my generation. When this crisis began, I consoled myself because I thought the social welfare structure could withstand this recession and keep the unemployed, the old, the disabled and the sick safe from corporate capitalism. After all, the social safety net had worked well for over 65 years. It had kept us safe during the violence of past economic storms. But during this tempest the government has refused to man the pumps, and now our ship of state is about to capsize. In one of the most perilous times in British history, the coalition government, with the approval of the Labour opposition, has introduced legislation that will eventually see large sections of the NHS privatised. The Health and Social Care Act will create a two-tier health care system. This act will see the NHS stripped down like a derelict house is for copper wiring by criminals.

UKIP has even proposed that A&E patients should have the right to buy their way to the front of the queue, while in Merseyside a private for-profit cancer clinic has set up shop under the NHS umbrella. Where will all of this end? What will be given the greatest priority in our new health care system that sends every service, from blood work to chemotherapy, out to the lowest bid tender? It ends where I began my life – in a Britain that believed health care depended on your social status. So if you were rich and insured you received timely medical treatment, while the rest of the country got the drippings.

One fifth of the lords who voted in the controversial NHS Health and Social care bill – which provides a gateway to privatise our health care system – were found to have connections to private health care companies. If that doesn't make you angry, nothing will.

Sometimes I try and think how I might explain to Marion how we built these beautiful structures in our society – which protected the poor, which kept them safe at work, healthy in their lives, supported them when they were down on their luck – only to watch them be destroyed within a few short generations. But I cannot find the words.

III. Brave new world

The circumstances that produced the British welfare state were remarkable to live through. I thought of this recently when I flew into Manchester airport on my way to Halifax.

It was early in the morning when my flight from Toronto entered British airspace. Outside of my porthole window the sky was cluttered with saturated rain clouds, which made me feel at home. In the distance the city loomed and below me its airport beckoned as the airliner made its final approach to land. I closed my eyes, tried to adjust my ears to the rapid change in cabin air pressure and thought about the first time I encountered a Manchester airport, in 1947. It was called RAF Ringway.

It was November, and to my 24-year-old eyes the nation looked anaemic and worn out because two years into the peace life was still as austere as during wartime.

The conflict had bled our country of men and prosperity, and now Britain shuffled on the world stage like a beggar at the entrance of a railway station. Like most people in Britain, I was uncertain about the present and nervous about my future. But I was still sure that post-war Britain was going to be a damn sight better for me than Great Depression-era Yorkshire.

Even with all the destruction that had surrounded me in post-war Germany, I didn't completely despair for the human race. I had faith that out of the ashes of war, something new was being built, especially at home in Britain. For me, nothing better exemplified the rebirth of our nation than the 1945 General Election. After all, I thought, it was the common people's blood, sweat and tears that had allowed Britain to survive the war; therefore it was our time to reap the dividends of peace. It was wonderful to be part of a great democratic renewal that was unleashed during that General Election. It was remarkable and unprecedented, but millions of British soldiers, sailors and airmen who had served in the war and were now stationed in military bases strewn across the Empire and in occupation zones in Germany and Japan turned out to vote and democratically determined the political fate of our nation. It took weeks for the vote to be tabulated but once counted it was irrevocably for Labour, and for a government based upon socialist principles.

While I was still in Germany, news about the struggles of life in early post-war Britain reached me through the wireless or newsreels that were shown every weekend to the occupying forces. Despite the war being over, the media still acted as a propaganda tool for the government. So we were fed an information diet rich in patriotism, bold political initiatives and the plucky resolve of the common man to face life's challenges with a grin or a thumbs up. There were stories about the proposed nationalisation of the coal industry, which caused many of my mates to break out into cheers because before the war they had been colliers enslaved by low wages in private coal pits.

Newspapers were provided to us by the NAAFI (Navy, Army and Air Force Institutes) and many outlined Clement Attlee's government's determination to replace 200,000 homes destroyed by Luftwaffe bombs with brand new estates. But I knew what anybody from the north, south or west of the country understood – that it would be a long time before we saw the slums in our neighbourhoods cleared and proper houses built for our communities. It was just a matter of arithmetic. Britain after the war was bust and therefore bombed-out London took priority over the rest of the nation. Letters from my sister Alberta confirmed my suspicions that the Labour government's desire to make our country a green and pleasant land for everyone was to be a long and difficult task. She wrote me and said that the looms in the mills across Yorkshire never stopped, not for time or tide, and work was available for anyone who was not afraid to get their hands dirty. However, my sister's news came with a few caveats: wages were depressed, inflation was up and rationing was still as vigorous as during wartime. As for housing, she wrote that neither love nor money could find you a decent place to let in the north. As my sister put it, all the money for new homes and flats was destined for the middle-class mucks down south.

Though the war was instrumental in changing the circumstances of our nation, it was also responsible for a great change in me. I cannot imagine that I was the only one, nor that the two things were totally unrelated. For the most part I had what is known as a good war, but near its end I was confronted by the horror of Nazi atrocities in liberated Belgium and Holland. Those images of the emaciated Dutch children are scorched into my memory and will stay with me as long as I am alive. I didn't think, as my RAF unit inched towards Germany during the last few days of the war, that my heart was big enough to forgive our enemies their transgressions against the inno-cent. That so-called 'turn the other cheek' Christianity just wasn't in me as we came to the burnt-out remains of Hamburg, Germany's second largest city.

When we began our occupation in the spring of 1945 the city's inhabitants greeted us with relief because we were not the dreaded Soviet Red Army. To many the Germans seemed tame and contrite, but I was not going to have any of it. In my mind their servile smiles con-cealed their past malice towards too many nations and races of people. For the first little while I treated these German civilians as suspicious and unworthy of my respect. It wasn't until my curiosity about their lives got the better of me and I began to learn their language and customs that I began to understand that most of us are innocent pawns thrown about by mighty rulers who have no respect for any moral authority.

As the months of our occupation wore on a famine began to plague the city which historians today call 'The Hunger Winter'. This sad and preventable tragedy created a lasting animosity between the victors and the vanquished. After I witnessed adults forced to survive on well under a thousand calories a day, I didn't blame those Germans who hated us. In fact, I was of the opinion that the longer we stayed, the more we became like every other military occupying force throughout the ages – we were just an agent to punish the vanquished and an instrument to exact war reparations through both legal and illegal means. During those years of occupation, as in Iraq or Afghanistan today, corruption was rife. On black markets the defeated German race bartered away their heirlooms for food rations, while in whorehouses young teenage German girls prostituted themselves and serviced members of the Allied forces to feed their families. Being in Germany broadened my perspective on myself and on society, because in that fire-bombed and horribly ravaged city I witnessed both the best and the worst that lurks inside every human heart.

As I sat on that plane in 1947, I knew that, no matter the uncertainty of peace, I was glad that Hitler was dead and the war over. As far as I was concerned I'd done my bit for king and country and served at His Majesty's pleasure in the RAF. In fact, because peace was still wet behind the ears I remained in uniform and did the air force's bidding in the German occupation zone. That was until I was seconded to RAF Ringway. When the world was at war, the airbase was used to train paratroopers for Special Operations, and afterwards its role didn't really change because the West and the Soviet Union were on the verge of armed conflict. So when I arrived at Ringway 65 years ago, there was a stark, warlike atmosphere that permeated the airbase and made my new mission for the air force seem absurdly punitive.

My superiors had transferred me out of occupied Germany and placed me at Ringway to command a squad of raw teenage conscripts in what I dubbed 'Operation Sisyphus'. Our duty, from sun-up to sundown, was to destroy thousands of RAF wireless transmitters and receivers with sledgehammers. Someone at the air ministry had deemed them surplus, and therefore despite their value they were destroyed rather than sold or stored for future use. For those recruits, the task was part of the square-bashing exercises. For me, however, it was punishment for entering into a romantic relationship with a German woman in Hamburg that led us to the marriage altar.

The post-war period was a confusing time to be young, because my generation grew up too quickly through the cruelty of austerity and the violence of armed struggle. Our hearts were callow to the ways of love, and yet we were cynical to the ways of the world because our innocence had been stolen from us by five years of conflict. Yet when the gunfire stopped and we marched into Germany, I knew that I didn't want to go back to being who I was before – a young man without serious prospects in life or love.

After the war, I wanted to make a difference somewhere, so I stayed on in the RAF and in Germany to help with their reconstruction. Besides, the air force was like home to me. I was fed, paid, treated well and had friends. It was a posting that allowed me to lick my wounds from a troubled childhood, and to recover from my peripatetic experiences during the conflict against Nazism. It allowed me to engage and learn from different cultures and realise that suffering is universal. Had I gone back to Britain straight away I think all the sharp edges that encased my spirit, my insecurities, my loneliness and my many other faults would have got the better of me.

My journey to become a more self-aware, compassionate person began while I lived amidst the rubble of a once great city. The injuries from childhood started to heal the day I met Friede. If she didn't save my life, she made it better, richer, more interesting and certainly more passionate. In 1947, she became my wife.

For 51 years, Friede was my constant companion, friend and lover.

The storms of war brought us together but at first we were not a good match. Our cultures, language and social standing were diverse. While I was working class, she was definitely from the bohemian side of town. She delighted in Mendelssohn and jazz, both of which had been deemed degenerate music by the Nazis. She could dance both the waltz and the jitterbug and found equal pleasure in quiet reflection with a book of Goethe's poems or at an all-night party held at a dance club on the Reeperbahn.

Friede had known turmoil throughout her childhood and adolescence. As a child who had grown up in the tumult of Nazi Germany, she never felt physically safe. This angst stayed with her long into our married life and even in Britain she suffered from PTSD symptoms.

How could it have been otherwise? She was the illegitimate daughter of a socialist in a country that despised and criminalised free thinkers. Friede's mother was a nonconformist too, but she had the same penchant for survival as my mum. After Friede's father left her, she chose her lovers more wisely. The next man she took to her bed and her heart was a local Hamburg businessman who at first collaborated with the Nazi government and then defied them by protecting a former business partner from the Gestapo.

When I met Friede, she was starving like the rest of Germany. Her legs were rotten with sores, her heart and nerves scarred by the brutality of war. She had seen the city of her birth obliterated by the RAF. Her psychological trauma was understandable because the city was now a silhouette of ruin. It was Gomorrah the day after God's wrath. Nothing in this modern world can compare to the intensity of death and destruction that Hamburg and its people suffered during the war years. During one three-day raid 50,000 civilians were obliterated by Allied bombs. The city was set alight by a firestorm that stretched for 22 kilometres. In one concentrated air attack the RAF and USAF killed more civilians than the Luftwaffe did in five years of bombing against the whole of Britain.

Like the rest of our generation, Friede and I were damaged goods. The deprivations of the Great Depression had affected me, and made me unsure of my capabilities. I hungered for acceptance, love and loyalty, but refused it on many occasions when it was offered to me because I feared its legitimacy. As for Friede, her pain came from living in the shadows of totalitarianism and experiencing the violence of war as a teenager. We were broken souls who found comfort in each other's arms. Like me, she wanted to live, to taste everything that was possible. In the beginning our love affair was furtive and tentative. We made love to each other before we learned to love each other.

Peace was for both of us a second chance, and we weren't going to let the opportunity of living a worthwhile life slip from our hands. We weren't going to fall into the same trap that had ensnared our parents. We weren't going to believe in the words of politicians. We would only believe their deeds. Besides, we had something else going for us – we were young. So we were going to rely upon our youth to give us the strength and the courage to carve out a new life that was different from our parents'.

But when I first met her the idea of love between an Englishman and a German was as contentious as same-sex unions are with some sections of society today. That is why I find it vexing when many people of today believe that my advanced age excludes me from understanding their aspirations to create a more inclusive society. In my opinion, they are wrong to ignore my history and the history of my generation. For I have an intimate knowledge about what it feels like to be denied the right to marry the person one loves. In a very small measure, I know what it is like to be castigated for choosing love over convention. To this day, it stings to think about the legal obstacles, the threats and the peer pressure that the love of my life Friede and I faced to be wed after the war had ended. During that time it was illegal for me or any other Brit to marry or cohabit with a German citizen. So I kept my relationship well hidden from my superiors or anyone I feared was callous enough to grass me up for being in love with a German.

Eventually the Labour government changed the law, and from August 1946 members of the armed services were allowed to marry former enemy nationals. Despite the abolition of the marriage prohibition, the military still tried every means to impede fraternisation between German women and British servicemen. I, however, ignored the dangers of falling in love with a German in a time of military occupation. My passion was so intense for my fiancée that I was the first member of the RAF stationed in Hamburg granted permission to marry a German. However, it would take close to a year for my marriage to be formalised, and during that period my future wife was forced to undergo humiliating physical, psychological and security examinations. I was told these measures were necessary to make sure that this German was an acceptable sort for British society. After my wife had struggled through these rigorous interrogations, I believed her ordeal was over. Sadly, I was mistaken, because I belonged to the Roman Catholic Church and they refused to marry us as the church deemed my wife immoral and not fit for communion. It was at that juncture that I accepted excommunication from Rome and was married by our RAF padre who told me afterwards: 'For both your sake and mine don't cock this up.'

I didn't, but the higher-ups at HQ thought I set a bad example for other members in my unit and three months after my nuptials I was sent to Ringway and slated for Civvy Street. After Germany, Manchester was a hard landing for me because it was the last stop before demobilisation and starting a new civilian life with my foreign bride. Naturally, I was apprehensive about my future because the job I had before the war (a grocer's manager – I had started in the trade as a boy when my family needed the extra money, so I understood it well by my teenage years) had been filled in my absence by a conscientious objector. So once I left the RAF I knew that I was on my own, and my choices were between sinking or swimming because there were no social services for vets returning to Britain. While I began my transition from humble but respected RAF LAC to ordinary unemployed, uneducated bloke from the north, I lamented the loss of security and purpose the RAF provided me with throughout the war and in its chaotic aftermath. At least while I wore my blue serge uniform I had food, a place to kip and a guaranteed wage at the end of each week.

When I was eventually demobbed and reunited with Friede in Halifax, getting a roof over our heads turned out to be an ordeal. When I approached our council office to see if there were any flats to let for returning servicemen, I was told that there was nowt going for tinker, tailor or soldier. In kindness, I was told that if we were in danger of living rough, the council was able to provide tempor-ary dormitory accommodation in the workhouse. In the end we made do in an unheated small attic space of my mother's one-up-one-down while I got myself sorted.

Still, I didn't feel utterly alone because most of my mates who returned from the war were in the same situ-ation as me. Our families might have survived the Great Depression and Hitler, but we didn't have anything to show for it except the determination to make a better go of it than our parents' generation did after the first Great War. As I scrambled to come to terms with post-war Britain, I started to feel that there was some reason to be optimistic, both for me and for the country's future. For instance, in 1948 the NHS was formed, and for the first time in my civilian life I went to a doctor's surgery and was treated for bronchitis with antibiotics that assured me a speedy and safe recovery. The cost to me was nothing, and I was grateful because at the time I was skint, having just started back in the civilian working world. As I convalesced, I was gobsmacked at the great consequences of free health care and the potential it offered to improve our society. It was a transformational shift in how we as a country viewed our fellow citizens. The creation of the NHS made us understand that we were in truth our brother's keeper, and that taxation benefits everyone through maintaining not just our roads and sewers but the health of our children, workers and elderly. To me, the introduction of free health care was the first brick laid on the road to the social welfare state.

But memories of Ringway vanished as I stood at the Manchester International Airport luggage carousel. Around me, people frantically texted on their smartphones or groused about the wait they were having to endure before their baggage was unloaded. The universal stress of travelling, familiar from years gone by. But there was something about their look that was different from that long ago time, when it wasn't a cliché to say that we were all in it together. Now, I feel that the glint of hope has gone from so many people's eyes because today's governments don't offer big ideas or new solutions to the horrendous economic inequalities that grow like moss over the face of the great structures of the welfare state.

At the passenger pick up, a distant relative of mine in his early fifties waited to take me to my hotel. As we shook hands, I remembered him as a teenager in the 1970s, when he lived on a desolate Yorkshire council estate. For him and his neighbours it must have been as grim and unrewarding as life was for the Russians who were forced to live in industrial cities in the wilds of the Soviet Union. He took my bags and made a quick joke about the sodden northern skies. We left the airport and disappeared on to the motorway towards the city of Halifax, which rests like a soiled penny in the palm of the Calder Valley.

On the way, he chatted with me about football and rugby matches and spoke about the rot seeping into Yorkshire: 'No one has any drive, or work ethic, there are too many scroungers, too many immigrants.' It was the argument that the tabloids have advanced every day since time immemorial: that there are always too many lazy poor people on this island wanting too much from hardworking taxpaying citizens. The more he talked, the more he sounded to me as if he were auditioning for a UKIP election pamphlet. Somehow I suppose he assumed that because I am a pensioner and a veteran of the Second World War I would share his intolerance of others. I am not surprised by this. Many people who are younger than me presume that because of my age I have a default setting which makes me, among other things, a lover of dogs, suspicious of immigrants, wary of welfare benefit recipients and distrusting of those who possess piercings and/or multiple tattoos.

As we entered the outskirts of Halifax, it started to rain. I longed to go directly to my hotel but my relative wanted to show me how much the city had changed since my adolescence and my first married years. Jetlagged, I let him drive me along soggy roads and laneways to addresses that I thought were best forgotten. Don't get me wrong, not all of my experiences in this city were negative or painful and I am thankful for the true friends I made while I lived here. But sadly all my mates from those long-ago days are now dead. So any time I return to this town, I am reminded about history's steady march onwards. It is only natural that when I visit Halifax now it makes me wistful for the vanished age of my youth, because despite the hardships I faced, I was young enough to believe in the prospect of a brighter future. I realise that once I am gone, there shall be no one left to remember those hungry days I experienced before the war. Nor will there be anyone to recall the frantic efforts my friends and I made, after the business with Hitler was done and dusted, to grab some happiness and meaning for our humble lives.

On our journey, I asked my relative how work was going for him. He paused for a moment to collect his thoughts. It was difficult for him to form a lifetime of disappointment into a pert Yorkshire stoicism but he tried his best, and said: 'Job's all right, I guess, for part-time labour, but that's all that can be got for a bloke like me.'

'It must be tough,' I responded. He lit a duty-free cigarette and laughed with a smoker's cough: 'No tougher than it was for you.'

I was quiet while I remembered my own famished youth, the General Strike, the breadlines and how much human potential was gutted by inhuman poverty and the greed of the ruling classes.

'It was a long time ago,' I said. I thought again what a miserable existence it had been for most everyone in the country. But after it was done and the war won, the politicians promised us that no one in this country would face that type of unemployment and helplessness ever again. So I really don't know why the Western world wants to go back to those bleak, unhappy times without a murmur of real dissent.

My relative flicked his cigarette out of the window and shifted gears as we came to a red light. 'Too long,' he said to me. 'There are so few people left alive from back then, you may as well be talking to them about the Black Death. Nobody recalls the shite in the 30s and that were fucking horrible. For Christ's sake, nobody wants to remember the shite in the 80s. It's all forgotten and swept under the rug by the newspapers and the BBC. They get nostalgic about the music, but they never want to mention the misery. It's all shite. As for the bloody Second World War, the politicians only talk about it when they need an excuse to go pissing about in one of those fucking Muslim countries.'

I must have looked crestfallen because he apologised and said: 'Look, here or down south, no one cares about the likes of me. We're just the crap that's fallen on the factory floor. The government and ATOS swept up blokes like me and put us into the tip with the rest of the day's rubbish. Those buggers don't give a toss for anything but their bloody money. I can bet you a pinch of salt to a pound of shit that once they have sorted out my lot, they're going to have a go at everyone else that isn't part of their gated fucking community.'

I grew silent because I didn't have any ideas as to how my relative could emerge from the murky depths of the semi-skilled labour pool. His story is unfortunately too familiar to this island. Still, it bears repeating because the bad luck of people like him has left a smudge on the soul of this nation. He was born in 1959 when it appeared that the country, after years of trial and error, had developed into an affluent and egalitarian society. Alas, it was a chimera, because by the 1960s Britain lagged far behind Germany and America in industrial output and GDP growth. So for my relative, along with the rest of the nation's baby boomers, their formative years were wedged between two politically unsustainable extremes: Labour's long winter of discontent and a new form of conservatism heralded by the ascension of the Iron Lady.

I wasn't surprised when he told me that the days he been on the dole equalled or surpassed the times he'd been employed. His story was the same as so many who lived in what was once Britain's industrial heartland. Not Thatcher, nor Major, Blair, Brown or Cameron ever tried to prepare them to face the challenges of working in a globalised economy that favours grotesque profits for the few over employees' right to fair wages and a decent life. My relative rattled off to me a string of jobs he'd held in mills and factories that were once famous for their productivity but were now derelict. His employment history read like a catechism to the north's obsolescence.

On our trip across Halifax, he appeared to shrug off life's disappointments until I mentioned Margaret Thatcher. My relative remarked sardonically: 'When I heard she died I went down to pub and celebrated with the rest of my mates. I can tell you that there wasn't a dry eye in the house for laughing.'

I don't blame him for not spilling a tear for our former Prime Minister. It is hard to mourn the passing of such a divisive politician. Too many people were at the sharp end of her stick when it came to economic, social and educational policies. After all, she had utter contempt for most people in this country. She despised the working class and the unions that fought to preserve their rights. Her politics were about division, and using the seven deadly sins to her party's advantage. Thatcher pitted region against region with policies like the poll tax that abused hard-working people. She unashamedly favoured her rich political supporters with patronage, while she balanced the treasury books with her policy of privatisation, at the expense of today's government. She was a tempest of hate that dismissed Nelson Mandela as a communist agitator, allowed IRA prisoners to starve themselves to death in prison and supported cruel and murderous dictators like General Pinochet because she thought she was a master of realpolitik. In truth, she was a deluded, self-aggrandising politician who sacrificed friends, family allies and most of the nation to feed her lust for power and prestige.

Yet I admit that politicians and their policies don't appear out of nowhere. Thatcher, who as you may be able to tell I have no love for, came to power because Labour couldn't or wouldn't deal with the serious economic issues that were threatening Britain's stability as a nation in the 1970s. In fearful times, voters will put their hopes in someone who promises that the trains will run on time and that taxes will be fair. Her vision of Britain is why we are in this mess today but ill-advised Labour policies assisted her ascent to power. In the end, my judgement of her was formed because I lived through her tenure as PM. I saw the damage she did to communities I knew and loved. I think that the best I can say about her is that in death, as in life, no one is ever ambivalent about her.

For a while as we drove, we were silent. Instead of talking or thinking, we listened to the windshield wipers. Near King Cross, we drove past a crowd of people queuing for a food bank to open. 'Poor bastards,' I said. My relative laughed and said: 'Nowt can be done but cry into our beers.'

'Perhaps,' I said, 'but it's still not right that a person who is in their prime can't make ends meet because the best they can do for work is a part-time job on a zero-hour contract. It reminds me too much of the 30s when men like my dad stood before the gates of factories and begged for a day's work, just so that their children might get something in their bellies before bed.'

Looking at Halifax today, I don't know what happened. I don't know what became of all those grand dreams and promises made to us by our leaders in 1945. What became of that vision to build a just and free society for each and every one?

I certainly didn't see it when I looked out of my relative's rain-spattered car window. Instead all I saw was the hurried despair of people who seemed to live from pay cheque to pay cheque. On the high street, once-familiar shops were shuttered or replaced by pawnbrokers who sought, as in the days of my youth, to turn wedding rings into grocery money. 'We pay cash for your unwanted gold' ran across an LED screen affixed to the shop window.

I cringed at the raw cynicism of the advert because it reminded me too much about my own family's experiences during the Great Depression when my mother pawned her 'unwanted' dress and my father's 'unwanted' Sunday suit because that was all that was left to trade for food. Once it was done and she had been given a few stray bob, she said to me: 'If the tides don't turn soon, it's the poor house for us.'

Back then, it was a hard business to stay alive but at least we didn't have to contend with the ubiquity and predatory nature of payday loan companies. It seemed they were on every street corner that we drove past that day.

'When did these all open?' I asked. It seems perverse to me that we have these loan sharks situated on Britain's ailing high streets and accepted by society as if they are businesses of stature. In fact they are the very opposite, because they are simply a means to bludgeon money out of millions of hapless people and keep them forever in debt and behind bad luck's eight ball through outrageous loans, fees and interest rates. I don't understand why people are not outraged at how these companies subvert the good name of commerce, because they are about as clean to me as a pimp or a money launderer.

'The world has changed a lot since you were a boy,' said my relative.

Though I didn't want to disagree with him, it seems to me that the problem is that it hasn't changed enough. The greed and hypocrisy of the toffs was rampant in my youth. But at least back then it wasn't considered a virtue, like in today's world.

The atmosphere in the car felt heavy and stagnant from too much talk about politics and the economy. I rolled down the window and stuck out my hand and felt the cold, hard rain fall against my cracked, old skin. I thought about the fact that it had been over 70 years since I first moved to Halifax. I came here from other parts with my mother, her quick-with-his-fists boyfriend and my two very young half-brothers for a new start. But that is another story.

All of a sudden my relative called out that we were on Boothtown Road and asked me if my mum had lived on this road. 'Oh, aye,' I said, but that was a long time ago. 'I bet this brings back fond memories, but it's changed a lot since you left because now it's filled with fucking Pakis.'

I am too polite, too tired and too much of a coward to tell him to shut his gob. But I don't understand his racism because throughout my life I have immersed myself in, and been enriched and amazed by, divergent cultures. In the late 1920s and early 1930s, my family and I lived in rough Bradford doss houses that were the last place of refuge for those whose financial lives were ruined by the Great Depression. In those down-and-out slums, we lived cheek by jowl with crippled war veterans, displaced pensioners, unemployed Irish navvies and Jewish families. I don't remember either the adults or children harbouring prejudices against our neighbours for their race or religion. Moreover, as a baptised Catholic, who attended mass in exchange for food, I was in a minority myself, but I was never abused because of my religion, except by those who preached it.

It wasn't because the poor were better human beings who were not capable of harbouring hatred for their neighbours; it was simply a matter of time management. When you are at rock bottom in your life you do not have the leisure to hate, because getting food and warmth is your prime occupation. That is not to say that prejudice did not exist in my boyhood, because it did, and it was more entrenched and blatant than today. After all, during that time Britain ruled three-quarters of the world and thought the residents of its colonies were about as fit for dignity and economic equality as it did its own homegrown poor, who lived in degrading and inhospitable slums in every city in the land.

'So what you think about your boyhood home now?' my relative asked. Painfully, I looked out of the car window on to this terraced-house neighbourhood, which appeared as forbidding and hopeless as when I first arrived after the war. I told him that if he meets me for a beer after I have rested, I will tell him about the prejudices my wife endured as a new Brit. I will tell him about the friends I made in post-war Britain who came from every corner of the world but ended up on our shores because of the rough storms caused by the Second World War.

My relative agreed that he would catch me up later, but

he still wanted to know about how I felt about Boothtown Road, in the here and now. I told him that when I was a lad, the people who kipped here were no different than the people who presently occupy this neighbourhood. 'In my day the people lived from pay week to pay week and never had enough to keep them safe if tragedy struck. They were slaves to the mill owners and got more grief than joy out of their existences. What little free time they had was spent down at the pub, the football pitch or on a church pew. Regardless of the great strides in technology and science, I don't think people's hopes and despairs are much different from my era, especially if you live in a neighbourhood like this. Look around you; these people must feel as trapped as I once did.'

After that my relative surrendered to my pleas to be taken to my hotel, opposite the station. As I closed his car door, he bid me tara and then drove off towards his home on a suburban estate.

For a moment, I stood outside the hotel and stared at the railway station across the street. All around me it was dead quiet but I remembered that when I was young this part of town was usually frantic with people because of the railway. Still, I recalled that there was a day in 1941 when it had been as silent as today. But that was a long time ago, and I had been going to catch the train that was to send me to war.

As I made my way to my hotel room, it occurred to me that the saddest thing was that if the boys I had known when I was a lad in Halifax – most of them killed in the war, or long since dead – who had hung around, poor, hungry, angry, with no sense of their own future, were to somehow be transported to 21st-century Britain, they wouldn't feel out of place. They'd fit right in.

Everything Old
is New Again

I. Education

Déjà vu, translated as 'already seen', is the phenomenon of having the strong sensation that an event or sensation currently being experienced has happened in the past. In these troubled times, it is what I live every day. I know what it like to lose loved ones early, to grow up with a father out of work, to see debt collectors come to your parents' door, to feel like you will never get an education, or hold a real job, or have a chance to find love and raise a family in stable economic times. I've been there, but I hope that future generations won't have to be.

When I think of my fortunes in life, I believe that what really turned things around was the opportunity I got after the war to further my education. In the 1940s, 50s and 60s, governments cooperated with business to enhance the prosperity of the nation. However, unlike today, it was under the premise that everyone must share in our country's success. That is why those governments from history invested so much public money in schools of higher learning, and doubled the number of institutes to 43 in the 1960s. They wanted to emancipate the working class from want and ignorance through education and ensure that the children of the middle classes had the necessary skills to navigate a modern industrial economy.

These investments had a phenomenal payout for our nation. Graduates from British universities increased from 10,000 per annum in the late 1940s to over 50,000 a year in 1973. State-sponsored institutes of higher learning have added to the wealth of this country, through producing expert professionals in science, medicine, technology, the arts and even business.

Friede and I didn't go to university, but in the 1950s we went to night school. Through adult education programmes I was able to improve my writing and comprehension skills, and further developed the love for writing that has stayed with me throughout my life. As for Friede, being able to take English language courses helped her feel more comfortable both at work and within British society.

Several generations ago, when urban renewal was the watchword for progress in Britain, the city council ordered the warren of rotting Bradford streets I once called home to be bulldozed to the ground. The bricks of poverty and the mortar of class division were turned to rubble by the wrecking ball of modern social development. A university campus was erected on top of unhappy dead-end lanes where my family once lived terrorised by unemployment, famine and disease. My boyhood neighbourhood was transformed from a ghetto to a scholastic paradise built on the premise that education was a human right for all of this nation's citizens. I saw the creation of Bradford University as a steel and glass testament to progress.

The university was constructed during an era of great social change and optimism for the future. In the 1960s regional and national governments weren't afraid to invest in both infrastructure and their citizens' well-being. Schools, council estates, hospitals, bridges and motorways were constructed at the same pace that the private sector currently erects condominiums in London's overheated housing market.

By the time students first began to enrol and attend classes in Bradford's university, I was long gone from that city. By the 1960s I, like so many other people from Britain, had emigrated with Friede to Canada to make a new start in a new land. I had left it behind me, but my sister Alberta was never able to break its gravitational pull. Work and her husband kept her near to our family's early tragedies. After the Great Depression my sister's life was fixed in an orbit that forever crossed paths with the struggles of our youth.

'You men have all the luck,' she said to me, after the war. 'If you're not going off to fight Hitler, you're moving on to greener pastures.'

I moved away from Yorkshire because I wanted to

put the past behind me. I didn't want people to know me as Harry Smith, son of a pauper, resident of doss houses and survivor of Bleak Times. I wanted to make my destiny without the baggage of my family's suffering to dog my career and poison my home life. However, I was never able to free myself from my early history, my parents, my sister and my half-brothers. They were in my blood, and a change in postcode wasn't ever able to erase what was bred in my bones, through tradition, fealty and suffering. Wherever I lived, for good or ill, I was still in my soul a boy from Barnsley who had grown up on the mean and desperate streets of Bradford and Halifax. Besides, my work with a UK carpet manufacturer required me to spend long periods of time back in Britain.

Nonetheless, during the 1960s I lived in a leafy suburb of Toronto called, funnily enough, Scarborough. I owned a back-split house that I shared with my wife and our three young sons, Michael, Peter and John. I marvelled that by the age of 40, I had travelled from the cruel warrens of Barnsley and Bradford to comfort of middle-class life. Yet it wasn't luck that brought me to this state of economic successes, it was government policy, because as in Britain, Canada had created a social safety net that protected its citizens from life's misfortunes.

In our back yard we had a mature pear tree that my boys climbed in summer and built snow forts underneath in winter. It was a safe place, and I was proud that my wife and I were able to create a loving and supportive environment for them to grow from boys to men. Sure, while they were growing up their knees got scraped, their hearts got broken and some of their dreams were dashed. But they were free of want, disease or ignorance. Their boyhoods were not stunted like mine by a daily struggle to survive during an economically depressed era.

The schools they attended in Canada were new, their teachers enthusiastic and decently paid. My salary ensured us a comfortable but not lavish lifestyle. I owned a second-hand Morris and we went to a country cottage for our annual summer vacations. It was an era that in both Britain and North America saw the urban landscape renewed by governments mandated to improve the health, education and living conditions of their constituents. While I may never have been able to free myself from the privations of my past, in those days it seemed that the next generation would be luckier.

Students today face many different challenges than what I underwent as a boy. Some of them I just can't understand, but others – the ones caused by the government's austerity measures that have diminished individual opportunity – I can appreciate. At home and abroad, many young people today are being blown off course from their middle-class destinations by the return of a monetised education system. Obtaining a university degree is no longer about having the right stuff to become a scholar; it's now all about the money.

The expense of education has got parents across this

country understandably concerned for their children's future. Over the last decade tuition costs have crept beyond affordability for most families. Except for the top 1 per cent of society, to make it to graduation day undergraduates must rely upon excessive student loans or their parents' willingness and ability to mortgage their retirement plans.

In the coming years, proposed government cutbacks in education subsidies will overwhelm the household budgets of many ordinary families. By 2015, when the education maintenance grant is set to expire and the National Scholarship programme is to be curtailed, uni will be an indulgence only for the wealthy.

Even today, the cost of higher education is punitive to a student from an average wage-earning family. In 2014, if you want to attend a British university, it will set you back £9,000 a year, or £27,000 for a three-year degree. By anyone's reckoning that's a lot of brass, and a big wager to make during a time of economic transition. Moreover, in the last five years, only half of those who graduated from a post-secondary institution found employment related to their field of study. Because of this nation's inability to generate sustainable job growth, many are in professions where their degrees make them overqualified and underpaid for their work tasks.

A university degree has become like a lucky dip on the national lottery: for every potential winner, there are countless losers. Yet there are few alternatives for the young. Seeing that unemployment for those aged 25 and under is at nearly a million people and underemployment affects millions more, it is not surprising that the young are so willing to put a flutter on their futures with a large student debt.

What is distressing is that no one in government or business wants to discuss or seek remedies to ensure that this generation is not sacrificed in the pursuit of a balanced exchequer. My greatest concern is that if students don't start to soon see demonstrable material and social results from the time and money they have invested in their education, our streets will be filled with civil unrest. If action is not taken soon to address youth unemployment and underemployment we may see riots comparable to the 1968 demonstrations that erupted on campuses around the world.

It is essential that we understand that this deficit between the cost of an education and its ultimate payout was not caused by young people having expectations that exceeded their grasp, as many media outlets like to report it. Instead, the problem lies squarely with our newly globalised economy that only generates profits for stock- and bond-holders and gives nothing back to ordinary folk. Young people are entering an employment market where both small and large companies won't pay a living wage to their employees. A national economy cannot be sustained when the cost of housing, energy, transportation, education and food strip most of its inhabitants of savings and require them to live on extended credit to meet even their basic household budget.

There is something patently cruel about this modern work world that demands a post-secondary degree for every entry-level position, but pays a salary that seems more commensurate with a school leaving certificate. Our university education system creates innumerable graduates who discover that the job market is not impressed by their expensive degrees. Only a minority of privileged graduates, because of their rarity and skills, get positions that pay £29,000 a year or more. As for the rest, they are condemned to an Ixion's wheel of student loan repayment in professions where wages have been hollowed out by this outsourced economy. It is a vicious cycle.

The young today are facing grave expenses caused by the need to have a post-secondary education to even get a step on the ladder of life. It will only get worse because the government plans to sell off student loans to private enterprise. In the not-so-distant future, graduates will face a daunting employment ladder while negotiating repayment of their excessive student loans to profit-driven companies that are as predatory as payday lenders.

For today's students, the hyper-inflated price tag of an average post-secondary degree education is a major impediment in their economic ascent to self-sufficiency. It saddles working- and middle-class students with enormous debts which impair their future prospects to build stable lives. Ultimately debt, an uncertain job market and the gargantuan financial burden of either renting or owning your domicile will cause unrelenting emotional stress that will affect the health and well-being of Britain in the future.

The angst of living in the constrained economy of today has created untold worries for students. According to a NUS study 80 per cent of those polled felt stressed from their studies. Seventy per cent were anxious over the precarious state of their finances because of their student debt, while one in ten had suicidal thoughts. This is not the future of 'education for all' that my generation dreamed of.

II. Crash

But then, vision in this modern world isn't about governments investing our tax money into the building of great societies; it's about tearing them down. In the name of efficiency, governments have delegated the shape and scope of 21st-century society to corporations, through privatisation schemes in schooling, medicine and the delivery of social services. Where once governments spent enormous amounts of money on maintaining our communities, our schools, our hospitals and urban and rural landscapes, they now advance it to companies in the form of subsidies, tax forgiveness or just good old-fashioned bailouts. Economists call it synergy, but I think it's just welfare for the big lads of commerce.

Last year, while the American people struggled through a desert of fiscal austerity that saw essential services disembowelled through budget cuts and its front-line providers decimated by employment attrition, their government gave more free money to corporations than it spent on the food stamp programme or on building affordable housing. In 2013 the Cato Institute estimates that the US government gave $100 billion, or 5 per cent of its federal annual budget pie, to US businesses in the form of subsidies. When it comes to feeding taxpayers' money to Wall Street and corporate America's fat cats the Democrats and Republicans are equal opportunity enablers, because under George W. Bush's administration subsidies paid to wealthy industries were $92 billion in 2006. In that same year, the American government paid only $56 million to fund food stamps and welfare payments for America's least affluent citizens.

These subsidies to rich corporations have humbled the United States' unwritten mission statement that opportunity to succeed should be available to anyone who displays the gumption to work hard and play by the rules. An egalitarian spirit cannot be kept alive in a country that subsidises the patrician class through tax revenue while everyone else is required to tighten their belts.

It is estimated that in the last ten years, $3 trillion has gone uncollected by the US treasury because wealthy Americans and corporations have shirked their civic responsibility to the republic by not paying their fair share of federal and state tax. This has contributed to the country's $642 billion fiscal deficit. Subsidies to corporations and their reluctance to accept a fair tax burden has prevented the US federal government from properly funding their nation's schools and colleges. It has stopped the government from keeping their roads and bridges in working order.

Collaboration between business and government that permits enormous amounts of public wealth to be transferred into the hands of private enterprise doesn't advance the public good. It is just crony capitalism that injures the free market and erodes society's fabric quicker than street crime denudes a neighbourhood of its real estate value.

Sadly, this 'I'll scratch your back if you scratch mine' relationship is not unique to Washington. It exists in Ottawa, Paris, Sydney and London. In fact, at the moment it seems that anywhere there is power, money fuels an all-encompassing moral indolence that leads to ethical corruption on an Olympic scale. Tax avoidance and subsidies to corporations is a massive septic tank leak that no one wants to fix. If governments and societies don't address its toxicity to the public good, it will seep out from the corridors of power and contaminate everything in its path.

It has already had a pernicious influence on our economy. During the course of the banking crisis and the recession that followed in its wake, the British government doled out roughly £500 billion to banks to keep them afloat. Just like in the Great Depression, both the

Brown and coalition governments rescued the banks and the well-to-do and made the rest of us fend for ourselves.

The burden for the financial crisis, like the economic catastrophe of my youth, was shouldered by the poor and the middle classes. It caused extreme hardship to the average taxpayer through job losses and a reduction in social services. Yet the wilful recklessness of the banks was never punished, nor did heads roll. No government sought to indict or persecute those responsible for a calamity that destroyed our economy and jeopardised our social safety net through feckless greed.

I was in the Algarve when the crash came. I didn't hear about it right away, because the neighbourhood in the small city where I resided was populated with expats who had come to Portugal to forget their troubles. Instead, it was by chance that I discovered that Wall Street and the City were on the verge of financial collapse.

I had gone to a café for my morning coffee and noticed a *Guardian* newspaper resting forlornly on the outdoor table opposite me. I scooped it up but I was hesitant to read it. I wasn't sure if I wanted to disturb my retirement with news from the outside world. Near me some local Portuguese men smoked and argued over the merits of a Benfica striker. It was a typical morning in the Algarve. The café's table umbrellas were unfurled to shield customers from the warm sun. The street was deserted, except for the odd tourist looking for cheap cigarettes. Everything was peaceful, normal, indolent and carefree.

Even the bright blue ocean looked calm and steady, far off in the distance.

I glanced at the headlines that told me of the Lehmann Brothers' collapse. At first I didn't know what to make of this financial news. I thought that surely there must be regulations, fail-safes, measures to rectify this? This wasn't 1929, after all. Surely our banks had matured in the seven decades that had followed that crash? I put away the newspaper and decided I was too old to worry about it. I thought it was best to go take a walk into the old town. I'd be damned if some banks were going to spoil my exile in the sun. You see, I had just moved to Albufeira. I had come, so to speak, to test the waters. I wanted to know if I could tolerate a cheap retirement in the sun.

I was 85 and a widower. My wife Friede had died ten years earlier from cancer, but during that time I had not been alone because my middle son Peter, who suffered from schizophrenia, lived with me. He was an artist of some repute but his mental illness required him to reside where it was safe, calm and familiar, and that was with me. Fortunately, after many years of therapy, his medication improved his standard of life and he was able to marry his long-term girlfriend. He moved away and I was overjoyed at his small step towards independence.

My son had suffered greatly from his affliction. So it was a great relief to me when he was able to pick up the strands of his life. I was glad that he was able to have a go at being an ordinary husband and homeowner. With him gone, I sold my home because I didn't want to end up cleaning my gutters every day to keep the dementia of boredom at bay. Portugal seemed the best answer to calm my wanderlust because it was a cheap and cheerful place for an expat to avoid winter's wrath. In summer, I came home to England and spent my days in Yorkshire.

At first, life for me in Portugal went on as usual. I read my books, I watched the ocean. Most mornings, I spoke to either my children or my grandchildren via Skype. In the afternoons, I drank wine in cafés near the ocean, made new friends, read books or wrote in my journal. I thought that if this was how my life was to end, it wasn't a bad note to go out on. But as the year progressed the financial news grew worse. In Portugal the government and the people seemed blind to the inevitable: 'There is no problem here in the Algarve. You Brits will always come and spend your money. Look, our cranes are still building condos, flats and timeshares. You should buy into one, because you can get a nice house for only 10 per cent down.'

On New Year's Eve, the coastline was lit up by a fireworks display which cost over half a million euros that neither the regional nor national government could afford. As I watched the festivities from my apartment balcony, I thought it looked more like an opulent distress flare rather than a celebration.

By February 2009 the good times were over for Portugal and most of the world. Coastal towns that had survived invasion, plague, wars, fascism and communism were now deserted of the commodity they needed most – tourists. Restaurants in the city where I lived were empty, especially the ones near the beach. Waifs with menus in hand desperately tried to pressgang me and the few foreigners still left in the town to enjoy a full English breakfast for six euros.

In winter, between school holidays, there were few takers, and it seemed that even the stray cats had moved out of Albufeira in search of greener pastures. As fiscal markets dried up, the *Telegraph* portended another Great Depression for Britain if Brown remained as Prime Minister. People started talking about their ruined pension pots, their fear of redundancy. The only reason I didn't was because I was struck by a personal tragedy that hit me with a ferocity that I had not known since boyhood.

My middle son, Peter, who had so stoically borne his mental illness, was diagnosed with idiopathic pulmonary fibrosis (IPF). It is incurable and in quick time it turned his lungs into cement. I returned home to care for him. Within six months, he was in hospital attached to a breathing apparatus that pumped air into his foetid lungs through a hose that had been cut into his throat. My boy, who had just turned 50, told the doctors he could take no more.

His death approached like it had done for my sister in 1926 and my wife in 1999; it came like a thug in the night to torture him. He didn't have an easy life, nor did his end provide him the tender mercy of an easy death. Instead, my son had to beg wordlessly to be no more, because the disease had stolen his voice. When he died, grief came to sit and brood in my heart. I was spent with sorrow. After Peter was cremated, I returned to Portugal and hoped that I would soon join my wife and son in death. Of course I didn't, because life never works out as you want it, even when all you want is to leave it.

Instead of dying, I began a spiritual odyssey of sorts. Having spent years running away from my past, I started to seriously explore it and tried to unravel the anguish that my generation endured before the creation of the welfare state. With the world around me collapsing, I came to the frightening realisation that the economic failure of 2008 was doing what the crash of 1929 had done to my generation.

Throughout the financial crisis, the government has reacted towards the banks like a co-dependent spouse when confronted by a weekend piss-up that caused a car wreck. It had taken a 'lads will be lads' attitude towards those who created the 2008 meltdown and the following recession, despite the disastrous impact they had on millions of lives.

Today, the dust still hasn't cleared from that disaster, and most executives in the City and on Wall Street only mention it with as much circumspection as former SS officers once skirted their responsibility in the holocaust: 'We were just following orders.'

Fortunately there are some in the banking industry that do see the crisis and how both the industry and governments dealt with it as a watershed moment for irresponsibility and a 'let's pass the buck' philosophy. One of them is Andy Haldane, the executive director for financial stability at the Bank of England, who admits that the bank rescue was poorly managed: '... what we saw was the upside being harvested by the financial sector and the downside being taken by wider society. That is unjust and wrong and intolerable ...'

Yet this social and financial inversion, where wealthy enterprises were shored up with government money that could have been spent on affordable housing, infrastructure maintenance, school and hospital budgets, services to pensioners and job training for the unemployed, persisted throughout the recession to other corporate sectors of our economy. When our economy was at its most fragile, our government provided £43.5 billion in subsidies to private enterprise, excluding tax grants. The money was given with little or no oversight to car manufacturers, arms merchants, the oil and gas sector, pharmaceutical companies and big agriculture. It was handed over without question or debate, despite the fact that our corporate sector had a cumulative cash surplus that was in the billions of pounds.

It was crass, inhumane, and malicious of this government to show no mercy to the unemployed, the disabled and the disadvantaged during the financial crisis. That it continues to behave like a bully to those down on their luck makes me think that the government's cruelty is deliberate.

They want to change society to reflect only the interest of our corporations and the 10 per cent of the population who profit inordinately from a system that chastises people, through lack of opportunity, for being poor or ordinary workers. Private for-profit firms like ATOS are used by the government to ferret out so called benefit cheats and malingerers, while the bedroom tax is used like a pike to keep the economically disadvantaged in line, through punitive cuts to their benefits or rent subsidies.

However, when it comes to the corporations of this country, garlands and cash are tossed to them for their fortitude in keeping the value of their shares strong through cost-cutting measures like job redundancy. Over the next few years, our exchequer is slated to hand out another £310 billion to industries that sit on a £800 billion cash surplus. Moreover, only one in four of these giant industrial oligarchies pays tax to the exchequer as they have created offshore havens for their capital. Obviously, the government has decided that the wealth and health of private corporations is worth more to them than the well-being of our schools, hospitals and infrastructure.

We worry about these things on a theoretical level, but for those at the hard end of society, I worry on a personal level. The effects of poverty can neither be over-stated nor reversed. As long as I shall live I will remember the cold I endured as a boy when I slept in an unheated garret with my sister, Alberta. We spent our nights there because there was no room in our parents' sleeping quarters for us. We slept in filthy rags and hugged each other for warmth. Sometimes my sister sang me to sleep in an effort to quell the hunger which gnawed at our bellies, while bugs crawled over our flesh.

In the morning Alberta and I would scrounge for food in our parents' room, but usually there was nothing to eat. So Alberta would go and beg for a slice of bread from a neighbour who was just as down on their luck as us. While I waited for my breakfast, I'd repeat the nursery rhyme: 'Old Mother Hubbard went to the cupboard to give the poor dog a bone. But when she got there the cupboard was bare, and so the poor doggie had none.'

Our poverty drove my mother slightly mad. She suffered from panic attacks and erratic mood swings. Mum didn't know what to do or who to turn to. Finally at her wits' end, she barked: 'One more day like this and it's to the poor house with ya, because I can't feed thee anymore. Better to be raised by strangers than your useless old mum.' My mum's angry pronouncements terrified both my sister and me. I was horrified by the idea that I might be sent away and imprisoned in a workhouse because my parents were at the end of their financial rope.

The 1930s were an unspeakably cruel decade for anyone without dosh or connections. The working class wasn't destroyed by the Great Depression; it was gelded by economic exploitation that returned it to the conditions of the 19th century. My parents' generation's desires for better living conditions, fair wages, better health care and schooling for their children were thwarted by politics and business that claimed the needs of the wealthy came before the rights of the many.

Our crisis in 2008 allowed today's political and business elites to enact austerity policies that were used to quell the rights of workers, limit environmental protection, increase the power of corporations to set the political agendas of nations and dilute the democratic process.

Unfortunately, there are too many people in both government and in business who believe that the wealth of a nation can only be judged by the value of its stock markets and the quarterly earnings of its corporations. This attitude negates the worth of human capital. It also denies what history and logic dictate – that a country has to maintain a balanced economy that includes manufacturing, agriculture, and financial services. It has to reward entrepreneurs with wealth for successful enterprises, but it must also maintain a decent standard of living for all of its citizens. There has to be access to health care as well as the right for everyone to receive a proper education, free of oppressive financial burden. Without those ingredients a country withers because it becomes a nation of two tribes: the rich and the poor.

III. Class

We have somehow forgotten our history lessons, because once again this country has this great social divide. We now have a nation that is unevenly split between those with wealth and those without it. Today our decision-makers and corporate mandarins live in a world that does not resemble ours. Except for their mortality, they would have us think that they are a more developed species than us. As the writer F. Scott Fitzgerald once said: 'The rich are different from us.' My mum, who had more than her fair share of encounters with the well-to-do, would have agreed with this, but probably would have added that the rich are crueller than us, too.

Poor mum, she always got the short end of the stick when she dealt with those above her station. 'As sure as there is church on Sunday, the toffs have got you dead by their rights.' My mother feared the indiscriminate authority the rich had over the poor. It was an understandable dread because in the 1930s they really did have the power of life or death over the humble.

Yet up until our descent into rough doss house living, my mother didn't consider her working-class background an impediment to having an enjoyable life. She believed that regardless of your station in life, each person was deserving of respect and human kindness.

I, on the other hand, felt dead certain growing up that nobody gave a damn for the poor – not the middle class, not the government and most certainly not the rich. They were so far away from our world of poverty that we resembled ants to them. To them we were a horde of vagabonds that camped at civilisation's kerb. They either feared us like we feared TB, or thought us less than human and undeserving of kindness.

As a child, I knew that being poor set me apart from the civilised world. My neighbourhood, the lack of proper sanitation, my clothing that looked like it had been woven with grime, all marked me out as a beggar, an urchin, an untouchable. My parents couldn't afford to kit me out, so I, like every other poor child in the country, was clothed by a charity. Since my mother had converted to Roman Catholicism (believing they had more of a Christian heart when it came to the poor), we were provided alms by the St Vincent De Paul's society.

I remember having to thank Jesus for his tender mercies before the nuns of my parish handed me a pair of filthy corduroy trousers which didn't fit me. It was out of the question to complain because I had learned early on that beggars can't be choosers. So I wore the clothes that displayed to the world that I belonged to the lowest social order – those on relief. Some of the more well-off children in school mocked me and the other poor students. They called us names, taunted us, chanted at us or ignored us.

On the few occasions when I travelled with my mum to the high street, it hurt me to see better-dressed children in patent leather shoes, while I traipsed along in my worker's clogs. They looked merry and carefree. It stung because I had the distinct feeling that they didn't see me as a boy like them. All they saw was a filthy animal, who was no more worthy of attention than a mongrel.

Yet still my mother believed that while poverty may have made us hungry and grubby, we were still English, British subjects, deserving of respect. 'We are just as good as anyone else,' Mum would say defensively to the pawnbroker, as she traded her wedding ring for quick cash to pay the rent and provide us with some meat for our tea.

Mum *was* just as good, if not better than most people. But her illusion that those with money or rank thought of her as an equal was shattered into unrecognisable pieces on the day she stumbled upon a department store's bank purse. She tripped over it on the pavement of the high street. It contained £50, which was a king's ransom to the working poor.

The money inside that bank purse would have remedied our dire straits. It would have stopped our spiral into malnutrition and ill health. It would have quelled our fear that we would be evicted for rent arrears and sent to live on the pavement. It would have prevented our descent into the nether reaches of destitution. My mum, however, didn't keep the money, because as she said: 'We were not raised to be thieves. We may be poor, but we're not bloody criminals.'

When my mother returned the money to the department store, the manager agreed that she wasn't a cutpurse. But he judged her not worthy of his time or his store's gratitude. As a fellow mortal, he judged that she was worth less than him because he saw that her dress was frayed and her hands dirty. To him, my mum was nothing because she couldn't afford to shop in his establishment.

Her honesty, her virtue, her belief in right and wrong was not valued to have any worth to him. So, in 'thanks', he presented her with a bag of broken day-old biscuits. Before she left the shop, he instructed her to 'make sure you share that with your family'.

From that day forward, my mum was adamant that the rich and those in power had nothing but contempt for those not born into privilege. Afterwards, no matter what strides occurred in society, she warned me that 'they will never give a toss for the likes of us'.

For a long while it was easy to dismiss my mother's jaded views about society. I reasoned that my mum was old and set in her ways. After all, by the 1950s the social welfare state was making my life and pretty much everyone else's more agreeable. We had health care, my wife and I lived in a comfortable flat in Halifax and although our wages weren't great, people's standard of living was improving enough to allow them to afford luxuries like TV sets and refrigerators.

As time went on, my mother moved into a council-subsidised flat for seniors. She had outlived two husbands and a lover and buried her two daughters. Yet no matter how she tried to evict the past from her consciousness, it always sat uncomfortably in a chair beside her. In her old age I should have been more sympathetic towards her uncertainty about being retired, but I couldn't be. We were both tortured by our experiences of the Great Depression, and it was hard to talk about those times.

'It won't last,' she said to me once.

'What won't last?' I asked.

'My bleeding pension. The government will find a way to take it back. They always do. Remember how they means tested your father for our poor relief and knocked off a ha'penny because they thought your dad was a wee bit high and mighty for their liking?'

'That's ancient history mum, best to let it rest in peace.'

'You're off your bike if you think I am going to forget. I'm no fool. That's why I've got a bit of booty stored away, so when they turn off the spigot, your old mum won't starve in the streets.'

'What are you on about?'

Her eyes grew bright and she said: 'Do you remember that money you gave me over the years, for Christmas and me birthday?'

'It wasn't much, Mum.'

'It was plenty, because I've got a hundred pounds squirrelled away in case they cut me off from my pension.'

'They can't cut you off, Mum, it's the law. Besides, they owe you a decent retirement.'

But she would not have any of it. I couldn't make her understand that she was entitled to a pension for the rest of her life. On that day, I knew my mum had never left the slums. They lay festering in her heart. As for me, I was now a grown man, married for 25 years with teenage children that were clamouring for designer jeans, driving lessons, or ski trips to Switzerland.

My house was almost paid off. I was well respected in my profession, which paid me a decent but not extravagant salary. The days of trouble seemed long gone for me, and, so I thought, for most everyone else who had lived through the Great Depression and the Second World War. I didn't want to relive them. So even though I was my mum's firstborn son, as I grew older we became estranged from each other because we both had survivor's guilt. We'd seen too much, and like those who have endured both the shipwreck and the desperation of fighting for our lives in the vast open waters, we couldn't emotionally accept what we had done during those dark hours.

Near the end of her life, I asked my mum if she was happy. The old woman, who was known as Mephistopheles by her grandchildren, bitterly roared at my naiveté. 'Lad, there are no happy days for our lot, because the lord mucks have got us in the palm of their hands. One squeeze and we're done for. Sod the lot of them. We're just fish trapped in their nets – we're tonight's tea.'

It's hard now to argue against my mother's world-weary assessment of society. We live at a very disconcerting period in history. It would be risible if it were not so repugnant that the minister for the Department for Work and Pensions, Iain Duncan Smith, equates his scorched earth policy against benefits claimants with the abolition of slavery. It is a deluded and callous time to be alive when the Mayor of London, Boris Johnson, believes that one of the greatest determinants of poverty is intellectual deficiencies, not the inherent inequity in our society. Perhaps that is why the capital now resembles a layer cake of wealth and want. The top is covered with rich icing and the bottom drenched in mould.

It is both anti-democratic and immoral when life doesn't get materially and socially better for the majority. It shouldn't be like that – I've seen this country in much worse shape than today, and yet there was still hope. It was an earnest optimism, not a slogan for a poster or a tag line for a political advertisement.

Long ago, we had a shared belief in our country that kept us defiant through the dark lonely days of the war. We maintained that unflappable determination even after we had won the war and were handed the bill for victory. We were in hawk to the international banks and to America while our Empire was on its deathbed.

I still remember what London was like after the war. It had been humbled by the brutality of the conflict and the austerity of the peace. Rationing and war debt had shriven the spirit of Britain. The blitz had been hard on our capital, but the peace was remorseless. Damage from the air war still littered many side streets, and polluted sleet gathered in bomb craters.

I had first visited the capital in the early years of the war. It was spring 1948 when I returned there in peacetime. The rain that came down was cruel, and the people looked glum. The weathered looks of ordinary individuals were understandable. After all, they had paid a steep price for victory – husbands, fathers, brothers and sisters dead from war in the air, on the seas and across the continent. It was a weary time, like today, but unlike our present those politicians from the past were hell-bent on keeping their word. They were willing to honour their oaths made to the people when our backs were against the wall. We fought on because our rulers had promised us a new deal and a new society if we soldiered on together against the threats to democracy. We don't have that now. All we get is talking point oratory from Westminster. Its rhetoric is hollow of intention and spoken with the conviction of a restaurant chain waiter reciting the evening specials.

Today, the gap between the rich and the humble is expanding exponentially, like our universe. Life expectancy for the poor is on average thirteen years less than for the rich in this country. Children who are from poor families are less likely to achieve five decent GCSEs. Not since the 1930s have government and business been so cavalier in their attempt to divide this country into economic tiers of opportunity. Profit is enjoyed by the upper echelons and financial loss is borne by everyone else. It is either a paucity of vision or greed that has corrupted their judgement.

It has affected our ability as a nation to face the social, technological and economic challenges of the 21st century. It has prevented us from engaging and being victorious as a people against the trials of modern life. Instead we have turned our backs on the future. Our leaders have attempted to return our society to the gas-lit streets of Great Depression Britain, when life was rough and ready for the poor.

It is so easy, in our present society, to ignore or misunderstand the lessons the past can teach us about today's world. Regrettably, popular television programmes like *Downton Abbey* make it more difficult for individuals to focus on the grave economic and political injustices that blighted past generations, or to realise that these wrongs threaten to eclipse the economic progress our country has made since the end of the Second World War. It may be a soap opera and considered light entertainment, but *Downton*'s depiction of our early 20th-century British history disinfects poverty and makes class prejudices palatable to modern audiences. It revises history to reflect an ideology that insists that wealth equals wisdom and virtue.

During my early days, the powerful maintained an unflinching belief that your social class determined your worth as a person and citizen. That is why in the 1920s and 1930s the families who ruled Britain believed that those of us who came from humble working stock didn't deserve anything but the most rudimentary education. We were like beasts of burden, only valuable in our ability to labour for the profit of others. Society expected us to follow into our fathers' footsteps and become miners or factory workers, but then the Great Depression had eviscerated every trade but soldiering. By the age of fourteen our schooldays were done, but the old professions of the working class were denied to us.

Sure, there were some lucky ones that went to grammar school, but they were the exceptions. The black hole of poverty, lack of social mobility and a rigid class system kept people like me scuttling across society's economic ocean floor. We all knew that whatever dreams we had for our futures were circumscribed by our past. Few dared to imagine living life outside of the villages, towns and tenements that had shaped their lives, their parents' lives and their grandparents' lives before them. From an early age, however, my blood was infected by wanderlust because my grandfather had been a soldier in India during the days of Empire. On the few occasions that I visited him, he told me about the far-off places he'd seen as an artillery man. It inspired me to dream of foreign, exotic worlds, and even when we lived in the slums I believed that I would one day venture beyond the walls of my family's poverty, and visit foreign countries.

My belief that I was destined to travel one day was encouraged by a First World War vet who was down on his luck and resided in our doss. He liked to tell me about France, the war and his adventures. The man enjoyed smoking cigarettes when he talked to me. When times were tough, he smoked strands of tobacco rolled up in Bible paper. 'The Lord works in mysterious ways,' he said, while blowing smoke rings up towards the ceiling.

When he was flush with money, which was rare, he bought Player's cigarettes. As a promotional giveaway, the cigarette packs contained small silk flags of different countries, embossed on cardboard. He liked to present these flags to me as a gift of hope. 'Nothing lasts forever,' he said to me with a shrug. 'The rain comes and it goes but it's staying alive until the sun comes out that counts. It makes it easier to get through the day if you remember that, lad.'

IV. Work

On the rare occasions when my mum wasn't blaspheming the austerity measures of Ramsay MacDonald's coalition government, she boasted to anyone that cared to listen that I was like a flash of phosphorous in a black coal pit: 'My boy, Harry, he's a wonder when it comes to knowing what's between the cover of books. Given half a chance, he could become a right good scholar.'

My mother's notions about my scholastic ability were based more on fancy than fact. At school, I was always behind in my lessons because during childhood my family were like early nomads, always in search of a safe place to eat and sleep. It was a lonely existence, except that I found pleasure, escape and enlightenment in reading books. My father encouraged this activity because libraries were abundant even in poor neighbourhoods and membership was a few pennies; another thing we are in danger of losing today. Dad knew that even if I did fall behind at school, reading would keep me from becoming dull and ignorant.

When everything else had been pawned or hawked, my father still held onto a leather-bound set of encyclopaedias called *Harmworth's History of the Ancient World*. They were replete with beautiful illustrations and photographs of the Egyptian pyramids, the temples of India, the Parthenon, and the Hanging Gardens of Babylon. My dad was always kind enough to let me leaf through them. For a small boy those books were like magic, because they transported me far away from the cursed life we led. I was able to let the books lead my imagination to places that were filled with mystery, beauty and wonder.

Unfortunately, whatever intellectual spark I had was savagely blown out by hunger, remorseless poverty and my class, which destined me to work as a horse in a shuck. Besides, by the age of seven our world had become a very desperate place. Much later on in her life, my mother said of those Great Depression years in Bradford that they were 'like being a rat on a sinking ship. No matter where you hid, the water was going to come and drown you.'

By 1930 everything that we had owned was gone to the pawn shop and my parents still couldn't pay the rent or put enough food on the table. At the time, my mother claimed that it broke her heart. 'Got no choice,' she said. 'It's this or the workhouse for us all.'

Shortly afterwards my mum had me indentured to the

local off-licence to work as a beer barrow boy. I was just seven, but adults couldn't find work. However, because there was no wage protection for child labour many young bairns were compelled to scrub floors, work in shops, push market carts, sell their bodies or beg in the streets to keep starvation from taking them and their parents to a premature death. For the children of my era, there was no alternative, it was a work-or-perish existence.

So after school until late in the evenings, and on weekends, I plied my steel wheel cart stacked high with ale and beer and sold drinks to the near-destitute who needed a bit of Dutch courage to get through the day. The few shillings I earned kept my family fed, but it broke my dad's heart to see his only son, a child, forced to work because factories and mills had stopped hiring men. I never knew how to react to my dad when I gave my mother my pay from the off-licence on Friday. Many times he tried to be absent so that he wouldn't receive my mother's rebukes: 'It takes a boy to do a man's work in this topsy-turvy world.'

But even though my dad was unable to find work, I didn't think any less of him. He was my dad and I loved him. I adored being in his presence. When I was in his company, my father impressed upon me his nobility of spirit. Thinking about that period, I am certain that he knew he would not be long in my life. The brevity of our relationship didn't prevent him from instilling in me a love for nature, for books, for civilisation and for justice.

On rare occasions, he took me on long walks in the park. During those strolls he told me about the history of England. He recited poetry to me, especially the sonnets of Wordsworth. He described to me the ancient wonders of the world and promised me that I would see and do marvellous things. He tried to make me forget the poverty of our life by diverting my attention through jokes, or by singing amusing seaside holiday songs. He loved football and recounted the exploits of his local club when he was a young man.

And even though times were rough, he tried to make the most out of family life. I remember the excitement of once seeing a Christmas panto, or going to the seaside with my family. I remember in particular one bank holiday outing to Southport. We went by bus from Barnsley to the coast. For my sister and me the ride in itself was an adventure because we had never ventured far from the coalfields of South Yorkshire.

At midday we arrived at the beach, which to me stretched beyond forever. Across the cold August sand I heard the sea roar, while above in a low, grey sky gulls darted and screeched. At first I was disappointed because the water was so far away.

Dad bundled me up onto his shoulders and marched me out to the land's end. With my sister and my mother nearby, we marvelled at the power and majesty of the sea. It was the last time that my family had a holiday together. It was the last time that we were all connected in a state of fun and relaxation; carefree and not afraid for our futures.

He was a man who tried to do his best and harmed no one. My dad was just knocked down by powers that were beyond his ability to control. Aside from enjoying a good pipe of tobacco, my dad's only sin was to want to put in a decent day's labour for a decent day's wages. He failed, like so many working-class men of his generation, to keep his family safe from poverty and ill health. However, it wasn't from want of trying but because the system was rigged against him. His sacrifices as a worker, man, husband, father and friend left me few tangible legacies. Yet, he provided me with an A Level on how to be honourable and decent, regardless of your economic station in life.

Many years after the war, when I was living in Halifax with my wife, two elderly women appeared at our doorstep. They had travelled from Barnsley to Halifax to inform me that they were my father's sisters and had come to give me my inheritance. I was told that on his deathbed, my father had asked them to flog what few possessions he owned and give the proceeds to me as my legacy for being his lad. One of the old women placed eight shillings into my hand. My father's worth at the end of his life was less than a pound, but to me his value as a father, protector and human being was immeasurable.

The last time I saw my dad alive, I was eight years old. There were 6 million men out of work across the country, him included. Children in Wigan, London, Cardiff and

Glasgow were starving, just like me. There was nothing my dad could do for his family, because he was like all of those other unemployed men put out onto the scrapheap of history.

My dad's remains lie in Scholemoor cemetery in the section for indigents. He wasn't afforded the luxury of his own plot but was buried in a mass grave for paupers. For decades my dad's bones have mixed forlornly with the bones of other men that were beaten into submission and death by the ferocity of the economic whirlwind dubbed the 'dirty thirties'.

For a long while, I had hoped that my father could rest in peace, like a sort of unknown soldier from an economic war that put an end to all economic inequality. Unfortunately, since the 2008 crisis, indigent burials have increased in Britain. It is estimated that over 100,000 people will not have the dosh to pay for dying this year. According to a report commissioned by the University of Bath, hundreds of thousands of people won't be able to leave provision for their funeral costs. Unfortunately, the £1,200 that the state provides for those families in need of funeral assistance still leaves many out of pocket to honour or give their departed a decent dispatch from this mortal coil.

It seems that our country has doubled back and returned to a period when the poor feared death because it brought more than grief: it left the living with a lifetime of debt.

The conditions under which I lived in those years, when there was no work for grown men and we were forced to subsist on the meagre recompense for my barrow work, affected me emotionally. I was constantly hungry, I had chilblains and I was constantly frightened that I would die in a workhouse like my sister Marion. Every night, I was tortured by bad dreams. My sleep was torment rather than an escape from our waking misery. The dreams that came to my unconsciousness mocked my desires to be free of pain and hunger. In sleep I flew with the grace of a kestrel and broke the bonds of my doss house existence. Alas, my nocturnal flights always ended when I woke to a gnawing pain in my stomach, the itch from insects on my skin and the sound of vermin as they scuffled with each other like pub brawlers along the floorboards.

We lived in a ghetto, so the other children I knew were in just as difficult circumstances as we were. Many worked, like me. Others begged, and many were abused both physically and sexually by unsavoury adults who always seem to populate poor neighbourhoods and prey upon the weak and the innocent.

After my dad was gone, my mum was grateful for the shillings I provided her every week. However, she knew that the only way we were going to survive the Great Depression was if she were able to find another man to replace my dad. My mother schemed to find someone who could become smitten enough with her to take on the responsibilities of our family. Unfortunately, my mother learned that in the slums it's hard to find a good man because everybody is scrambling to stay alive. Eventually, Mum took up with an Irish navvy who was good with the craic and little else. He got her pregnant and then cleared off for Australia.

When I was seven and a half, my half-brother Matt was born, and there was another mouth to feed. From that day forward, I knew that my responsibility, whether I liked it or not, was to earn money to keep my mother, my sister and my brother alive. It wasn't childhood for me, it was penal servitude. In rain and snow, I pushed the barrow while my mother became unhinged by poverty. She started to drink and her tongue became a fierce weapon to battle against anyone who crossed her. On many occasions, I fell upon her unhappy fury.

Sometimes, mum crossed the line between cruelty and abuse. Once, in the company of strangers, she tore one of her breasts from my brother's feeding lips and doused my face with her milk because I had demanded her attention. I cried in shame and she replied: 'What's the matter? Ain't you hungry?'

While my mother found comfort in the beds of strange men who she hoped would find it in themselves to do the right thing and make her a respectable woman, I found respite at the library. There, I devoured the novels of Hugo, Dumas and Dickens along with the plays of Shakespeare. While I read to escape the grimness of my world, my mum eventually entranced Bill the pig man.

He was not much of a catch, but he fancied her and tolerated us kids when he was sober. He tended hogs and swine and thought more of them than humanity. He was required to travel across Bradford in a horse-drawn cart, collecting slop from restaurants to feed his herd of pigs that was housed in an industrial farm, several miles north from our ghetto. Sometimes on his rounds Bill collected giant mounds of congealed sweets from a toffee factory. 'The little buggers love pudding just as much as we do,' he said with a coarse laugh. When he was in a good mood, he would give my sister and me one of these football-sized masses of toffee. 'Go on,' he said, 'have a go at it. It's better than Blackpool rock.' So my sister Alberta and I would attack the congealed ball of toffee with a makeshift cricket bat and smash away until we found an edible portion to sweeten our bitter existence.

In 1937 I turned fourteen, and I was in my final term of school. We had moved from the slums of Bradford because Bill had found work at a rendering plant in Sowerby Bridge. When that didn't work out, we tried our luck at King Cross. Finally we ended up in the Boothtown Road area of Halifax, in an uncomfortable, noisy and run-down tenement. We occupied it with relief mixed with trepidation because our luck was like milk: it soured easily. It was a cramped, dank house that felt as overcrowded as the doss because it housed me, my mother, Bill and my two younger half-brothers, Matt and my mum's son with Bill, William. Alberta had cleared off as soon as she had found full-time work in a mill located not far from Low Moor, in Bradford, and I didn't blame her.

It was in Halifax that Bill began work as a butcher. In a small outbuilding located some streets away from us, he gutted animals of dubious provenance and let their blood flow into the stream out back. To those who were hard up he sold offal, udder and ox bone. When business was slow, he inflated pigs' bladders and played football down the lane.

My home life was still unstable because money was tight, and my mother and Bill liked to row both in sobriety and in inebriation. However, my wages as a delivery boy for a local grocer had stabilised our finances enough to ensure that we always had food for tea.

I was at an age when it was expected that I don a worker's cap full-time. I enjoyed school but I was under no illusions; I was destined for the working world because my kind weren't made for apprenticeships or university. Still, my mother believed so much in my academic capabilities that she bought me a Latin grammar book: 'Son, it's the best I could do for thee, but books will be thy torch out of this warren.' In the end she was right, but at the time the people of my class were supposed to follow in their father's footsteps. My dad was gone and I had no relation that wanted to take me under their wing and teach me the ropes of their profession.

Still, I wasn't too worried because my resumé was chock-a-block with experience. More or less, I'd been earning my keep in the grocery business since the age of seven. I didn't need a soothsayer to read my destiny: I was going into trade. It was all that I knew. How to lift, how to bike, how to push, how to deliver, and how to smile and be deferential to my betters.

My sister Alberta loaned me the dosh to buy an ill-fitting second-hand suit to look for gainful employment, and I was quickly hired to work the cheese barrow for Halifax's Grosvenor's Grocers. It didn't pay much, but the other employees were kind-hearted and showed me how to do my job. I learned my duties and my place. I began my transition into the adult working world, like everyone else had in my class since the age of Victoria – with grim acceptance that this was the way of my world.

While I pushed giant wheels of cheese from one end of Halifax's commercial district to the next, I knew that to get ahead in that world I had to change my past and my background. I enrolled in a Halifax institute called the Athenaeum, which had been established by socialist cloth-cutters in the 18th century to better the lives of the working poor. I took courses in elocution to improve my diction and wash away the harsh tones of my northern dialect. 'Can't get anywhere in business,' I was told, 'if you sound like you should be mucking out pig shit rather than living in clover.' So, I cleaned up my accent and took courses in composition and book-keeping. Over time I became one of the managers in the grocery shop.

My later teen years were not tragic or as sad as my

boyhood, and I have education, as well as hard work, to thank for that. Work, my courses at the Athenaeum and the general improvement in the economy gave me the confidence to make friends, go to dances and woo local girls. It was a typical working-class introduction to young adulthood. Back then I thought I'd do all right if I could get the scratch to move out from under my mother's roof and find a girl to marry me.

If it hadn't been for the Second World War and the revolutions that came after, this might have been all I'd managed. I became a man before the birth of the social welfare state, and the debt of being from the wrong social class could have kept me and my contemporaries down for good.

Even now, I can't dispute that the poverty of my youth has branded my personality and my outlook on the world, for good or for ill. It could not be any other way, because the Great Depression was a cataclysmic occurrence for most of my generation. Few lived through it without being scarred by its brutality. People lost so much in the 1930s: jobs, homes, families, wealth, and also their dignity. It was a long time ago, but you never forget it. Nobody I knew in my life ever really freed themselves from the trauma extreme poverty created in their spirit. It damaged so many people from my generation and ruined their lives. It shattered any hope for them of finding happiness in later life through family or friends. How I survived it without growing bitter, I will never know, though I suspect much of it was because I found love and pursued a stable family life over material riches.

V. Hunger

Over 80 years of time and tide separate me from my early history, but it still has a hold on me that I cannot completely escape. The war, marriage, children, a career, retirement, grandchildren – nothing has displaced that singular, pervading loneliness and helplessness that hunger and family discord generated in me as a boy.

It was hard to watch my father be beaten, worn, and eventually washed away by the tidal surge of the Great Depression. He was never able to get back on his feet and, since his demise meant our end, my mother shoved him out into the sea of homelessness. There was no choice, but it stung. The night she told my father he was yesterday's news and had better move on, he took it stoically at first. My sister and I might never have known that my mother was abandoning my father to feed us children, except that dad in the end broke his quiet resolve.

In the hours when doss houses are quiet because the residents are exhausted from cheap drink, hard work and the realities of dismal prospects, my father began to wail like Lear over his lost kingdom. He screamed, he shouted, he cried at how he had been forsaken. At first my mother tried to bark down his roar of despair but he would have none of it. He called her a slattern, a cheat and a bitch.

Mum laughed at his accusations and cut him to the quick. 'You've left me no bloody choice. I've got to look for a man who's got work, who's got brawn, who's got brass. Love's got nowt to do with it. It is about staying alive in this ruddy crooked world.' All of a sudden his rage turned physical. He drew his pocket knife and threatened to kill his wife. She laughed and he charged at her but he was subdued by his own decency. My sister and I found him huddled on the stairwell sobbing to himself over his jilted life.

The next day, in mercy or as testament to her love, mum gave me half a crown and told me to buy two ounces of roast beef at the butchers. 'It's for your dad's tea,' she said sadly. It was the last time we sat down as a family and ate a meal together. While we gorged on bread and dripping and my dad tucked into his meat and tried to keep his dignity, my mother looked weathered, older, harder but unbroken in her resolve that she and her children would survive and damn the consequences. From that night forward, my sister and I knew that everything – love, honour, decency and life – was to be sacrificed in times of great economic duress and famine.

As I aged, a scab formed over these horrific experiences of youth. It is only natural; everyone has to crack on through the muck and mire and hope that sunshine returns to their community and their own personal life. Today, however, those emotional and physical wounds I suffered as a boy are being picked open by the great unravelling of our society and economy.

This new age of austerity has created so much personal and financial uncertainty that social media is rife with fear and indignation. However, there is one persistent motif that runs on Facebook timelines and twitter feeds across the country – it is that hunger has returned to the side streets of Britain.

Yet despite overwhelming evidence from the media, charities and individuals that food poverty, like a tidal flood, has begun to encroach upon both city and suburban dwellers, the government remains unmoved. In fact the coalition has myopically ignored this economic deluge which has engulfed vulnerable communities and demographics in the same way they ignored the ocean gales that placed coastline villages and towns in jeopardy at the beginning of 2014. Apparently the steps to mitigate the dangers of flooding or eradicate famine are considered too costly during an era of fiscal responsibility.

To our current leaders prudent foresight is irrelevant. They act like acolytes from a cult who worship corporate profits over common sense. To paraphrase Oscar Wilde, when you put a price tag on owt, you don't know the value of nowt. But I can tell you that society pays a heavy cost when it allows its youngest to be denied an education and future prospects because of poverty and hunger. Such inequities build resentment, class hatred and distrust between the generations. They divide and pit region against region. It creates cynicism and animosity between workers and managers. Ultimately, it ruins the social contract that binds a people together as a nation.

In the 1930s such divisions almost ruined Britain because back then destitution or near poverty affected every member of the working class, which was the majority of the country's population. However, instead of political upheaval, a consensus was reached between the working and the middle classes in the 1940s which led to the birth of our modern welfare state.

For over a generation, British society worked together for one common aim: measured prosperity for everyone. To achieve it, free health care and education were provided to every citizen to even out the playing field of life. Its motive was both idealistic and practical, because in the end it permitted Britain to compete economically in the industrialised 20th-century market place.

Therefore, in this modern age, all citizens should be alarmed when the charity Children's Society has documented that over 3 million British youngsters go to bed hungry each night in cold, damp houses infested with mould. Moreover, everyone should be concerned when 49 per cent of teachers have reported that some of their students are beginning to show noticeable signs of malnourishment. We must remember that these statistics are real children; members of our community whose present misfortunes will affect our future economy and society.

Unfortunately, the current Secretary of Education doesn't see a connection between poverty and

under-performing state schools in disadvantaged neighbourhoods. According to Michael Gove, it's not food
poverty or an increase in economically pressed children that
threatens Britain's education system but its teachers and
their union. Gove believes that state schools must emulate
fee-based institutions and return to teaching a curriculum
that promotes our imperial heritage and Anglican faith, and
favours the skill of technocrats over creative disciplines.

The Secretary of Education wants teachers' salaries
to be based upon their performance as instructors and
determined by the exam results of their students. This
proposed method would reduce teachers to pedagogical
assembly line workers whose wage is set by the amount of
widgets created rather than in the craftsmanship it takes
to produce an educated citizen. Gove's belief that competi-
tion by schools for the best students and best teachers will
improve our overall education system is not only erroneous, but would prove lethal to our state-run schools. All
it will encourage is the flight of our best human capital
to private institutions.

For those who are not blessed with wealth or excep-
tional intellectual talent, their schooldays in this cruel
new world will be remarkably similar to mine. They will
be taught the modern-day equivalent of my syllabus,
which was to know your sums, be literate enough to read
instructions, docile enough to know your place and most
importantly have a strong back to shift coal.

Systemic poverty prevented me and many from my

generation of even getting even the fundamental education the state provided us. Poor relief was less than a pound a week for a family of four. Rickets, TB, malnutrition and mental illness stalked everyone in the slums like a bird of prey. The times were so primitive there weren't school lunch programmes. I had to learn the law of the jungle before mastering the multiplication tables.

Back then hungry children were as common as pennies because the government of the day believed that austerity was the great cure-all to the Great Depression. Inevitably the young, ground down by extreme hunger, became feral. On Britain's mean streets we hunted for food like stray dogs do now in third-world countries. As a child I remember scrounging through restaurant skips in dingy back alleys on my way to school. To survive, I dug through the rubbish of other people's meals to find discarded fruit or meat that could sustain me until teatime, when my family generally supped on bread and dripping.

So when I found out that the British Red Cross has been forced, for the first time since the Second World War, to resume providing food parcels to destitute families, it enraged me. No, I felt more than anger: I felt my kind had been betrayed by a younger generation that had put their personal wealth over national prosperity. Over this past winter, Glasgow City Mission had to close its food bank because it ran out of supplies for those who were in need. The demand for subsidised food is so great that the Trussell Trust expects that they will disperse emergency food supplies to over a million people in 2014. It is an overwhelming statistic. I don't think the average person wants to imagine that multitude of hurt. People's lives are complicated, and so if we are not directly affected by a natural disaster or economic tragedy we try to avoid mention of it. Poverty, wretched living conditions and unemployment can be found in every part of this country. But we tune it out like static on a radio.

Despite the fact that we can locate people in desperate economic circumstances in all of our neighbourhoods, we sometimes don't think it is real until we see it on television. Unfortunately, we can sometimes take TV personalities like Katie Hopkins, who earn their brass by demonising the poor and creating false stereotypes about those on benefits, as experts on economics or the human condition. Yet these voices that ring so loudly are media creations, and only exist to create discord, mayhem and hatred, and in turn to increase the television company's viewing figures and revenue from advertising.

Today, so many of us refuse to accept the truth that the majority of people on benefits would rather be building a sustainable life through employment, rather than just keeping their heads above water on the dole. However, this Poundland economy where employees are expected to exist on minimum wages and no benefits makes it hard for those on welfare to get on with the basics of their lives, such as getting a roof over their heads and getting enough to eat.

VI. Cheap talk

We live at the sharp end of history. The average person today is at serious risk of losing their livelihood and their lifestyle. No one is immune from unemployment, and too many are just one pay cheque away from insolvency.

According to Shelter, the homelessness charity, one out of every 106 homes across the country was under the threat of eviction or repossession at the end of last year. That's over 200,000 residences. In the East London borough of Newham, one out of every 35 households was at risk of eviction. The lives of too many in Britain are ruled by financial uncertainty. Whether it is fear of eviction, economic strain caused by wage restraints, clawbacks in benefits, the bedroom tax, fuel poverty or the food poverty that has forced many families to trek from one food bank to the next like prehistoric hunter-gatherers, it has caused serious structural damage to the fabric of our society. It threatens to impede the proper emotional and educational development of our children just as the Great Depression did in the 1930s to my generation.

It was a long time ago, but the political rulers of today speak like those politicians of old. In times of doubt and crisis the tone is always similar, no matter the century. In my youth, a coalition government asked that its working and middle classes tighten their belts to speed Britain's economic recovery. We were asked to be patient and told that the jobs and the wages would come back. We waited through many winters, springs, summers and autumns, but recovery never came. Jobs, stable wages and decent housing didn't actually materialise until after the Second World War. It was at that point in history that prosperity began to return to Britain and the modern welfare state was created.

As in my youth, today's politicians utter like a catechism that both full employment and better wages are only a matter of letting the business cycle run its course. Their pronouncements are the same carnival barker's cry that I heard in my boyhood: to be patient and endure economic suffering and injustice because it is the patriotic thing to do.

President Obama, David Cameron, the Australian Prime Minister Tony Abbott and the Canadian Prime Minister Stephen Harper all read from the same hymn book and sing that the economy has recovered, but that it is as fragile as blown glass, so don't expect much if you are working or middle class.

The question our leaders don't want to answer is: 'For whom has the economy recovered?' It is certainly not for the average wage earner, the student or the pensioner. The sad truth is that the majority of professions haven't seen substantive wage increases in 25 years. Moreover, those raises were predominantly geared towards upper- and middle-class occupations, while those in working-class jobs did not enjoy similar bounties.

I admit that in the 1970s and early 80s I was lucky, and survived with little discomfort, but the average bloke who worked in a factory, shop or mill was hit hard in both decades. Hyperinflation and labour unrest created a financial instability that produced Thatcher's Britain. The country wanted stability, but the price we paid was unemployment levels that skyrocketed to Depression-era levels while whole regions, communities and industries were decimated by policies of privatisation. In that era, Thatcher's conviction that a free market unfettered by regulation would return Britain to its former mercantile glory was as near-sighted as was the left wing's refusal to accept that capitalism does produce benefits to the individual and society at large if properly controlled and cultivated.

During the economic and social discord in Britain in the 1970s, I travelled to Germany with Friede to visit her ailing mother who lived in Hamburg. In that city the campuses and the streets were sometimes filled with disgruntled citizens protesting against injustice that they wanted to eradicate in their communities. Looking at the protestors, I wondered why Germany was not confronted with labour unrest like Britain. The answer was apparent when I became reacquainted with some of my wife's distant relatives. They came from all walks of life – some were bankers, some were skilled tradespeople and some were managers, while others worked the assembly lines of Germany's greatest industries. Each agreed that Germany's success was built upon certain key elements: cooperation, mutual respect between managers and workers, a belief in non-adversarial methods to air grievances between those who ran a lathe and those who managed a company's books. What I learned was that Germany had created an almost perfect system of work where profits were shared, problems solved through mutual agreement rather than discord, and workers had pride in their ability to create good quality products. No one felt that they were better than the other; each person understood that their efforts built a better a company and a better life for themselves.

During the Second World War, Britain had those qualities of cooperation, fairness and mutual respect in both the business of war and in the service of work. It is pity that in the 1970s workers, the middle class and industry lost their empathy for each other because that was what made us great.

Many of the people I had known in my youth suffered greatly in the 70s and 80s. Their lives had remained fixed in Halifax and they remained tied to their working-class professions. For them, both the winter of discontent and Thatcher's political and economic revolution were seasons of bitter disappointment. It was a time of self-reflection about the value and the meaning of their sacrifices in the Great Depression and during the war.

The summer of 1977 was the last time I saw the mates of my youth all hale and hearty. After that year, one by one, my boyhood friends began to die, until the last one shuffled off this mortal coil in 1993.

But in August 1977, I was 54 and though we were no

longer larking about and chasing girls around town, my mates were still in fine form. As we had grown, married, moved on and had our own families we had drifted apart physically, emotionally and even politically. However, since our friendships were forged in the difficult days of the 1930s we were united forever by our past struggles in a hard-knock world. We might never have articulated it, but we loved each other and rooted for each other's personal success during days that were both thick and thin.

I will always remember the last evening we were together when went to watch Halifax Town AFC play a forgettable match in the Edwardian Shea Stadium. We sat on seats made of stone, drank Webster's green ale and smoked Rothmans cigarettes. In between taking the mickey out of the players on the pitch, my friend Roy, who had been in the Guards during the war and had seen combat in Italy told me: 'I don't know what it's all about any more. It's all cocked up.'

It was a tough time for Roy because he was a factory worker and although he owned a house, his wages were being eaten away by inflation. Crime was up all across the country, and it looked to him like civil society had had its chips. My other friend, Eric, who had been in selective service because he was a skilled tool and die maker, told him not to fret 'because the unions are just getting what's due to their members, after years of being beat down by Tory governments.'

Doug, my other mate from that long-ago world, also

worked for a union shop. But he wasn't as convinced as Eric about the crusade of the unions during a time when the country was in debt and bills had to be paid. He had his doubts, and moreover he was growing afraid for his future and his retirement. 'If we don't get a handle on these strikes, ordinary folk are going to go off us because this country is a right bloody mess. I think Labour has lost its way because it is no longer about the working man, it's about the egos of the union bosses.'

When the match was over and we pushed our way through the same turnstiles that had been around since I was fifteen but were now rusting and dilapidated, Roy looked over at me and said: 'You've been as quiet as a mouse when we've been nattering on about politics. That's not like you, Harry.'

'Oh aye,' I said. 'I was just thinking that things are bad today, but they're not for me. Not like how it was in the past. I'm worried about how everything is changing and getting mucked up. But I feel lucky. I can pay my mortgage, I can pay for our groceries. I can even take holidays with my wife. Besides, my lads are healthy and my oldest is at uni – that's more than we could have ever hoped for. And I know it is a bit of a worry for you, but your house is paid for and retirement is nearby. Your daughter's done her schooling and now has a right good job. It weren't like before, because we have better housing, the NHS and real universities that the working class can attend and make something of themselves in.'

'Too right,' he said.

After that, we went off to the pub and forgot about politics. But for the rest of the evening, in the back of my mind, I was fearful. Why? Because despite what I'd said, I knew from history that extreme economic and political discord is bad for society. I also knew that people crave stability and they will settle for anyone, regardless of their merit or worth, who promises them calm waters, low taxation and a return to the straight and narrow. Life was all right for me at the time, so perhaps I was just letting the wider problems of the country slide by me.

Crikey, that was ages ago. How I wish my friends had survived as long as me, because I really miss their friendship and their laughter.

By the 1980s I was in my sixties, preparing to retire, and I was chuffed for myself and my family. My children were all grown. My eldest had married and was beginning a family, my youngest was finishing up at university and my second son was working as an artist and theatre set painter, despite the difficulties of his mental illness. Personally, it looked like it had all worked out for me. I had survived the Great Depression, found love and risen to the middle class. Yet, on the horizon were all of the telltale signs that this was not to last, because Margaret Thatcher was the Prime Minister of Britain and Ronald Reagan was President of the USA. Those two conservative leaders and their cadre of neo-con supporters saw society very differently than my generation did. Reagan and Thatcher espoused an ideology of smaller government, less taxation and more input by business leaders rather than the interest groups of ordinary citizens. It was, in short, a revolution against the welfare state. Battles were fought to castrate unions in both America and Britain. In the US, the air traffic controllers were fired and in Britain Thatcher went to war against the north, its mines and a union that had sought to protect the livelihood of a region.

We couldn't prevent it from happening, but people still protested and made a last-ditch attempt to save society from those who wanted to make civilisation exclusive to the rich. Students and unions protested in the streets against the gradual erosion of the welfare state. However in the end both Reagan and Thatcher won their revolutions. Today not even mainstream left-wing politicians like mentioning the benefits of the welfare state versus our increasingly monetised public service.

Too many people in Britain are struggling with food poverty, fuel poverty, and rent poverty that it can't be just ascribed to a 'cost of living crisis'. It ceased to be a crisis when the recession stopped wage growth and caused cutbacks to social services. Now it is more akin to an income catastrophe, where the well-to-do seek to feather their nests on profits created by the suppression of fair wages. To talk about recovery when consumer debt is at an all-time high, manufacturing output in December 2013 rose by only 0.3 per cent, unemployment remains above 7 per cent, 21 per cent of young people are out of work and

250,000 people under the age of 25 have been out of work for over a year seems to be more than premature. It is misleading.

It is a question of credibility. How is it possible for legislators to talk about recovery when they speak without understanding the real misery that austerity has caused to 21st-century society? How could they really know what ordinary folk feel? In this and every other developed country, our members of governments' net worth always exceeds the average, from cabinet ministers to ordinary MPs. They are statistically always part of the top 1 per cent of society. Besides, even if they come into government with modest means, they always leave rich.

Considering the hardships that have been endured by the poor and the sacrifices made by the middle classes since the 2008 meltdown, there has been little compassion offered by governments to their people. Instead, every Western country in their parliaments and senates has voted for austerity over comprehensive tax reform, because the latter would affect their corporate friends' bottom line. For any MP or newsreader to say that we are on the mend is about as reassuring as someone who is colour blind telling you the light is green.

But it is little wonder to me that Westminster is disconnected from ordinary people in Britain. All you have to do is take a look at where these people went to school. Fifty-four per cent of Conservative sitting MPs received their education at fee-based schools, like Harrow or Eton. If you factor in Liberal Democrats and Labour, the number of MPs who attended independent schools accounts for a third of the House of Commons' membership. Outside of government, in the world of plumbers, joiners, accountants, technical workers, doctors and lawyers, only 7 per cent of the population attended fee-based schools last year. In fact, this number of public school boys guiding the ship of state hasn't been this prevalent since the days of Empire. Considering that the average tuition fee for Eton is £30,000 – more than the yearly wage of most citizens – and that David Cameron likes to surround himself with his 'old boys', how truly representative can this government ever be of ordinary taxpaying citizens?

Honestly, I don't know if they can represent the values I learned through a lifetime of working, raising a family and paying my taxes. My values weren't formed on the playing fields of Eton. They were formed by experiencing the cruelty caused by the Great Depression, and forged by service to my country in the RAF during the Second World War. My values include both sacrifice and sharing. My values are framed by the idea of a welfare state that is not just compassionate but prudent. I find it ironic that many right-wing commentators and politicians find fault with certain immigrant minorities because 'they don't fit in'. Ostensibly these newcomers cling to their ancient traditions and don't assimilate into our British way of life. Perhaps they don't immediately, but over time people always start to assume the attributes of their country.

In truth there is only one exception to this rule, and that is the students who attended private or fee-based schools. The parents of the majority of those attendees want them to be separate from the rank and file of society. They want their children to be welcomed into a clique that bestows upon them the ancient traditions of privilege, rank and segregation by title or material wealth. The ones who don't fit into our society are not the new migrants, but the old families and the nouveau riche who adamantly believe that they and their progeny should rule Britain for their sole material benefit.

Many of my fellow classmates who attended those tough schools of yesteryear shared my values and beliefs. However, none of those schools I attended in Barnsley, Bradford or Halifax ever produced a prime minister, a lord or even a humble backbench MP. I know that the failure of those schools to produce a member of the green benches was not, as Boris Johnson would have you believe, because those students lacked talent. It was because they lacked opportunity.

The Green and Pleasant Land

I. Frost

In the sparse, afternoon daylight I look outside my kitchen window to see winter brooding like a disgruntled old man. These long, dead months are hard on my weary bones. But unlike so many young and middle-aged people who are struggling through this dark, cold season, I at least am able to keep myself warm by a fire. My government old age pension that I earned from a lifetime of contributions to the National Insurance scheme still protects me from reliving the fuel poverty my generation suffered when we were children.

In this day and age, however, too many of us have been affected by weather extremes created by man-made climate change. No country has been spared the wrath unleashed by our carbon footprint. This year Britain was assailed by historic ocean storms and gales which raided our coastline and flooded hinterland communities with the cruelty of invading Norsemen. In North America, snow and frozen rain broke free from their arctic ice barriers and stormed across that continent, shutting airports, motorways and businesses. Nature, bridled and enslaved by us, has begun to rebel. And it has sent a chill down the spine of the world's fragile economy. In 2014, the cost to clean up UK communities which were inundated by seawater and swollen rivers will be in the billions.

The Prime Minister attempted to reassure the citizens and businesses that were harmed by these floods that when it came to the repair, 'cost was no object'. It is a pity, then, that neither this government nor previous Labour administrations have displayed real-time wisdom to protect agriculture and coastal communities from disasters caused by climate change. Instead, the Department for Environment, Food and Rural Affairs has seen its budget reduced by £500 million since 2010, and must reduce its budget by a further £300 million by 2016.

It is sadly ironic that as a nation we are so keen to be vigilant when it comes to a nebulous war on terror or drugs, yet when climate change or systemic and dangerous income inequality threaten our society, we choose to ignore the hazard until our counties are inundated with water and our neighbourhoods are eroded by poverty. Whether it is nature's fury, or an ongoing economic crisis, we ignore these harbingers of doom at our peril.

Around the world, present-day governments rely too much on the services of PR firms to turn financial and natural disasters into pyrrhic victories that are devoid of reality. I can tell you – because I was there – that Britain didn't win the Second World War by employing spin doctors. We were triumphant because everyone from low- to high-born was willing to sacrifice their time, their skills and even their lives to ensure that democracy was victorious over the evil forces of Nazism. It was not an easy period to be alive because both soldiers and civilians died in their thousands, rationing was in effect and the home front was assailed by aerial bombardment. Yet, when the smoke lifted from the battlefields of Europe and Asia, not only did peace return to Western democracies, but social justice was also introduced to the lexicon of free people.

After the Second World War, for the first time in our nation's ancient history, Britain became a green and pleasant land. The social welfare state envisioned by the 1944 Beveridge Report and implemented by the 1945 Labour government was as revolutionary to 20th-century governance and society as the Magna Carta had been hundreds of years before.

The social safety net produced the NHS and a national housing strategy. It regulated transportation and core national industries to be responsive to the free market, its customers and their employees. The education system was democratised, slums were cleared and modern sanitation was introduced to many communities that in the past were deemed too poor to deserve indoor plumbing.

These achievements in social progress created an economic boom that allowed Britain to attain a GDP growth of 5 per cent through the 1950s and keep its unemployment rate at a manageable 1.6 per cent. Conservative Prime Minister Harold Macmillan was right when he said in 1958 that 'we'd never had it so good'. The social welfare state protected the country from the horrors of endemic poverty or ill health, and it propelled the country forward. By the 1950s and 60s our young, regardless of their class, received a comprehensive education that allowed them to navigate a job market that required employees to be familiar with changing technologies in shipbuilding, steel manufacturing, mining and factory assembly lines.

It has to be remembered that the social welfare state was not constructed during fair-weather days, but at the end of the Second World War. The costs to reconstruct Britain's social and industrial infrastructure were enormous, but it was done. We built this new society while repaying the billions we borrowed to wage war for democracy's survival.

The social welfare state was created with prudence, foresight and was paid for through enlightened taxation. The government levied an income tax that was progressive and fair on both individuals and corporations. The rate was high: in some instances 50 or 60 per cent. However, we must not forget that for over a millennium the richest families of the realm, along with their industries, hoarded their wealth and paid little or no tax to keep the ship of state afloat. History teaches us that when taxes were not properly levied slums flourished, epidemics raged and crime was rampant. A two-tier society, cruelly divided by prosperity and poverty, was created. When the welfare state was born, the government and many of this country's inhabitants agreed that paying tax was a civic responsibility.

Britain's economy and society advanced towards the future with the speed of the *Flying Scotsman*. This new, incorruptible tax code gave our nation the fuel we needed to achieve the economic velocity to propel Britain into the modern world. The national economic success was created by providing our citizens with affordable housing, health care and education. Even Conservatives like Winston Churchill acknowledged its benefits to the country, and he refused to dismantle the NHS when he returned as Prime Minister in 1951. After the war, our nation lived for decades in what seemed like perpetual summer, where the needs of the individual were protected while our economy was nurtured through free enterprise and state encouragement.

But now, when my life is near its end, the great garden that allowed our society to flourish free of want, ignorance and poor health has grown fallow from inattention and crass politics. Perhaps that is why I couldn't bring myself to attend any New Year's celebration this year. I decided to defer my congratulations over the death of 2013 and the birth of 2014. Too much has happened over the last five years, I thought, for me to wear a silly hat. There is just too much economic anguish out there for me to pretend that everything is all right in this funny old world.

In fact, everything that was old seems new again. It is all becoming as familiar to me as the back of my own hands.

II. Home

It is hard for me to fathom that in a world of smartphones, TomToms and stem cell research 38 per cent of children in modern-day Manchester and 33 per cent in Liverpool live below the breadline. Where once prosperity was shared, the new mantra is every man for himself. Even in Europe, which is known for its generous and fair social welfare policies, one in seven is on the verge of destitution.

Every state is rushing to embrace the injustices of olden days. In the United States, where once there was the New Deal, now there is a raw deal for anyone that is not part of the elite. The streets of America are no longer paved with gold but strewn with the abandoned hopes of anyone who got caught in the economic tsunami of the subprime meltdown.

Although New York is a city of immense wealth and culture, it is overwhelmed by a subculture of poverty. Today, there are 22,000 children in that metropolis who have no fixed address. Not since the days of soup kitchens and hobos riding the rails has the Big Apple seen such pornographic disparity between the rich and the hopeless. Popular folklore once claimed that this city never slept. To be blunt, I don't see how it could in good conscience, considering that some of its most destitute areas are reminiscent of the Bowery in 1933 or the slums of South America.

It is not much better here in Britain. According to Crisis, the homelessness charity, homelessness has become a clear and present danger to the fabric of our society. Last year in England roughly 113,000 people in need were barred from the council accommodation waiting lists. It is estimated that there are over a million people who are part of the hidden dispossessed, those who don't qualify for council benefits or can't receive benefits because of austerity measures. With no fixed abode, these unfortunates shift, weekly or nightly, from one friend's couch to the next. But they are still luckier than those who live rough in London – a demographic that has increased by 62 per cent since 2010.

No doubt it is these facts, combined with remembering my own rough living as a lad that contributed to my distemper over this year's New Year television extravaganza. In the end, it seemed to try too hard to reassure me and everyone else watching that all was well with Britain and the world. Cameras relayed back to me a constant reel of well-dressed, rosy-cheeked revellers in Sydney, Beijing, Moscow, New York and London.

At the stroke of midnight, I heard Big Ben herald the end of one time and the start of the next moment in our history. As the clamour subsided, my TV screen was suddenly alight as £1.8 million worth of fireworks exploded above London's darkened skyline. The exhibition appeared to me to be an exercise in derisive triumphalism, rather than a celebration everyone in the capital and country could enjoy.

As the cascade of explosives over the city grew brighter, I began to think about all those inhabitants of London who are forced to live below the lights of celebration, in the shadows cast by the excessive lifestyles of the 1 per cent. It is so hard for the ordinary shop and office worker to get by on their stagnant wages which cannot keep up with this country's punitively expensive rents. It is hard to make do when access to government services has been diminished by privatisation and cutbacks. For many their life has become circumscribed by a scrawny pay cheque. This has led them to live a roundabout lifestyle where credit cards or payday loans offer temporary and illusionary relief against the expense of living in a modern society.

When the war was done with Hitler, my generation had great expectations. We wanted our society to be more inclusive and equal. Despite the cost, victory in war had made us exultant, and so our demands to our political leaders in peace weren't humble but revolutionary: we wanted a life that was enriched by education, by love, by family, by community and by employment.

In many ways, existence was even more complicated than today because the Great Depression and the war had dislocated so many people's lives. People couldn't just brush themselves off and return to the old ways. Our country had to deal with a surge in refugees from Eastern European nations that were now under the boot of Soviet domination. After the war, Britain had a moral commitment to grant rights of settlement to over 300,000 former Polish soldiers. They had to be trained for civilian life, taught English, and provided with housing. Yet it was done and few complained about our responsibilities to those who had helped us win the war.

We were fortunate that we had elected a government intent on rebuilding our cities and industries, so there were jobs for anyone who wanted to work. The pay might not have been great but it was steady and it kept you housed, fed and entertained. Housing at first was hard to come by but at least landlords didn't try to take excessive profits because of the shortage.

Moreover, the post-war Attlee government was committed to redressing economic and class inequities that had clung to British society like barnacles on an aging boat. In short order, Westminster directed that a million affordable homes were to be built across the country to house returning soldiers and their families. Some were just simple prefabs banged together quickly, but they had four walls, a parlour and two bedrooms. It was more than most of us who lived through the Great Depression could have dreamed of. A mate of mine who had a young family was overjoyed to be allowed to live in one of those government-built houses after he had done his wartime service in the Pacific. In those days, the government wasn't just building houses; it was in the business of helping its servicemen rebuild their civilian lives.

Today, the housing crisis in the UK is as dire as it was after the Second World War. Yet there is no cohesive policy to combat the shortage of affordable housing or the dangerous growth of inflated house prices. Austerity's paper hanger, George Osborne's Help to Buy scheme, has according to many analysts been an abysmal failure. Albert Edward, the head of the global think tank Société Générale has even gone so far as to say that this policy has aided and abetted the housing bubble. According to him it has caused young homebuyers to become indentured to mortgage debt that is spiralling out of control.

Unfortunately in London, as in Toronto, Vancouver, New York and Berlin, wealth and well-being is tenuously maintained by a delicate housing market bubble. At the moment, it soars buoyantly above reality's stratosphere, but like the Dutch tulip bulb market in the 17th century, it has the potential to burst and cause fantastic devastation to the world's economy.

I have only owned two houses in my life. The first one my wife and I bought to give us some space and comfort to raise our young family. The second one we bought for our retirement on the proceeds earned from selling our first house. For me, owning those houses gave me peace of mind because I knew that they could be used a fund for a rainy day, or as equity for my wife if I died before her. Before we owned a house we rented and lived in either rooms or flats. In the early years of our marriage we had to live at first in my mother's tenement, and then we shared accommodation with some friends of ours. When we were young and looking for digs, we wanted several things: affordability, easy access to public transport, clean and safe surroundings, nearby parks and a sense of community. At the end of Friede's life, I was happy when she told me that she loved me, and had enjoyed every minute of our time together. But she also remarked that even when our financial situation had been tight, 'we always lived in nice places that were pleasing to the eye.'

Wanting a nice place to live isn't something exclusive to my generation. Today's young people desire similar things when it comes to housing. However in this age, trying to check off all the boxes that make one's living quarters a place to call home has become almost impossible for the average person starting out on their life's voyage.

III. Memory

Lately, in the mist between sleep and waking, I hear in my mind Blake's ancient hymn, 'Jerusalem', sung during the war by me and my brethren. I stretch out my hands and try to grab hold of the images of myself as a boy and as a young man in the war, which play in my imagination like a newsreel loop. I hear fragments of popular songs from youth: 'Brother, can you spare a dime?' that mix with wartime melodies: 'We'll meet again, don't know where, don't know when ...'

In my dreams I am haunted by the breadlines of my youth and the rabid hunger that devoured my soul. I am dogged by the words and deeds of politicians who brushed off the demise of civilisation through austerity policies during the Great Depression and ignored the rise of Nazism in Germany. But I am also assuaged by my memories which are filled with grand times and extraordinary friendships and loves. Although I have endured much hardship and sorrow, I have also experienced wonder, joy and happiness. Even in the darkness of the Great Depression I remember light reaching and igniting my soul. The love of my parents and my sister. Sitting on my dad's shoulders watching a football match we couldn't afford tickets to. Peeking into a circus tent with Alberta. And later, punting down a river in Somerset during RAF training, and drinking beer and smoking cigarettes in a nearby field. Marriage. Children. Grandchildren. There have been many bright spots in my existence.

Most of all, there is one image that remains with me in both my waking and sleeping hours: it is that of Friede. I will never forget her face, her smell, her caress or how we kissed and pined for each other when we were young and separated by the rules that forbade our love affair. Still, it turned out all right; our wedding day was a glorious event because I was able to provide a feast for her malnourished family and friends. We were able to share our love and good bounty with those we loved. It was magic, and that we had over 50 years together still makes me one of the lucky ones.

It was an eternity ago, but for me it was like yesterday. The post-war years were chock-a-block with so many simple moments for me and my wife, alone or with friends. Everything was fresh, sometimes difficult, stressful and frightening but beautiful because we were young and healthy.

I have been lucky, because despite the hardships of my youth, I was granted the chance to snatch a life from the rubble of economic ruin and war.

I am calmed by recalling that there was a time when our needs were met. Some of my friends from boyhood stayed for ever in the council flats, content with their manual labour jobs and their annual trips to Blackpool in summer and during the illuminations. Others moved on to points far and wide on the map, but they were still protected by a society that believed in fair play when it came to housing, health, schooling and fair wages.

Today things are very different. Now it is always about the rich and powerful cutting deals with other titans. It is always about making common people pay for the mistakes of our rulers, either through a decline in living standards or through our blood.

IV. Appeasement

When I was a teen, our Prime Minister Neville Chamberlain appeased a tyrant and championed class division through his government's legislation. Today most politicians, regardless of the slant of their ideology, are in the business of appeasement; but now instead of feeding the lust of tyrants they bow to the monsters who rule the corporate world.

In September 1938, few understood that Chamberlain's Munich Agreement irrevocably doomed us to war with Hitler. But today, economists, historians and newspaper pundits generally agree that when France and Britain placated Nazi Germany's demands for territory in Czechoslovakia, it emboldened Hitler to build a totalitarian empire from Western and Eastern Europe's timorous skeleton. Ultimately the failure of Western democratic institutions to act concurrently and decisively against the dictator doomed our world to a war that saw over 60 million casualties.

It is lamentable that lessons about the dangers of appeasement have not been learned. Modern political institutions are quick to build moral equivalents for wars against the tyrants of our political epoch if it suits our ideology or economic aims. Suez, the Falklands, Grenada, Panama and Iraq are prime examples of wars conducted and justified by drawing erroneous parallels to Hitler and his very real threat to democracy.

In this day and age, presidents and prime ministers say too often for the television cameras that they 'will not appease dictators'. Perhaps not, but those who sit in Whitehall or rule at the White House are very apt to pacify presidents of hedge funds and corporate board directors by offering bailouts to banks too big to fail. Governments have mollified giant corporations like McDonald's and Walmart through subsiding their company's paltry minimum wage payments with food stamp programmes. Politicians appease Google, Apple, Amazon and other megaliths that act like medieval city states by not creating stringent, irrefutable tax codes that target those companies or wealthy individuals who seek to bury their wealth offshore. These companies may not be breaking the law, but in my view the law is erroneous.

In Canada and the US, the oil and gas lobby is given free rein by all political parties to overwrite environmental protection legislation when it comes to the extracting, refining and transportation of crude oil from the toxic Alberta tar sands. In Britain, despite the documented dangers to wildlife, the water table and human beings, fracking has been given a green light to drill in environmentally and seismologically sensitive areas.

Each time governments offer tax breaks and environmental deregulation – without due diligence, proper oversight, reasonable checks and balances, financial subsidies – to corporations whose sole objective is profit, social democracy is placed in jeopardy.

Every instance, every example, every precedent where governments have turned a blind eye to corporate maleficence or allowed their social services to be monetised and put into the absolute control of private enterprise repeats

Chamberlain's folly at Munich. There can be no peace or economic equality in our times if power is concentrated in a handful of individuals or corporations.

It is terrifying that in a world of 8 billion souls, fewer than a hundred men and women control half its wealth, thereby having enormous influence on its politics. In Britain, wealth is similarly concentrated at the top. According to Oxfam five families control 20 per cent of this nation's wealth. Money influences politics and the way our governments rule us. That is why the Cameron government gave a £3 billion tax cut on pension contributions to this country's top wage earners this year. The ordinary person may gripe, groan and whinge about their burdens, but the rich have the ear of our legislators.

The people of Britain, the Commonwealth and the United States did not go to war against tyrants in 1939 to allow 85 people out of billions to be granted the riches of Croesus. If we do not curtail our blind obedience to a metastasised system of capitalism that overrides environmental protection, human rights, national self-interest and human decency, it will imperil more than democracy, it will threaten the survival of our species. We must remember the City is not the nation.

V. Light and darkness

Recollections for me are like pin pricks – they smart with the vibrancy of youth. They draw to the surface how much has changed in our world and how much is disturbingly similar.

In the days that followed our declaration of war on Nazi Germany, I sat in my mother's tenement and heard the King's speech over the wireless: 'In this grave hour, perhaps the most fateful in our history ...' While he spoke there was silence across the low and high streets of our island. Afterwards on our quiet stoop, I shared a cigarette with my mum. She rarely smoked but thought she needed something to calm her nerves. 'It's out of the frying pan and into the fire for us lot,' she said wistfully, and then went back inside to make us all a cuppa.

When France fell to Hitler and the battered expeditionary army languished on the beaches of Dunkirk, I was just seventeen and still wet behind the ears, at least according to my mother. But like everyone else from my generation I wondered whether we'd be forced to fight them on the beaches. Could Britain hold out against the dark forces that had subjugated Europe?

In the beginning of the war, the claxon ring of air raid warnings was thrilling, surreal and bloody good fun. Then one night the laughter stopped. Death came abruptly, as it had come for Guernica, Warsaw and Rotterdam. This random murder came from above, and it came to us each and every night – a tempest of explosives and incendiaries thrown from the belly of German bomber planes. Like the endless rain, misery fell on London, Sheffield and Hull. The indiscriminate bombed streets of Britain smouldered for five years until peace was declared.

While the war was on, strict rationing was imposed, national security cards issued, a propaganda ministry was created and civil liberties were curtailed. However, in those days there was no panic amongst the population, only resolve to get on with the job, to keep buggering on until Hitler and his Nazis were dead and buried.

The government promised its people that if our country survived and was victorious in this war, our rights and freedoms would be restored to us. No one doubted the need for vigilance during this war because it was a universal battle between good and evil; it was the last war where one was able to see clear distinctions between right and wrong. We didn't need government officials to mislead us into thinking that we were in danger, like they did with Iraq. We didn't need an American government to create false threats of WMDs, because our war against Hitler and the Nazis was a true battle between democracy and crass dictatorship. It was not a battle for oil or corporate spoils. It was a struggle between light and darkness.

We knew, when war broke out, that the time for sowing and reaping was over. We had come of age and had to renounce our youth to become soldiers, sailors and airman. It was our time to defend the state against the darkness of dictatorship. On a damp February day in 1941, I left my mother's house and began my induction into the RAF. Before I departed my mum implored me to keep my head down, because 'life even in peacetime is too bloody short, lad'. I walked away from the cramped tenement house of my teenage years and rode the rails from Halifax to Padgate where I became a man.

During those first few days of square bashing, excitement and fear danced cheek to cheek in the imaginations of us raw recruits. As I learned to march, salute and obey my sergeant major's bark to keep my eyes right, I knew that the air force was a damn sight better place to be than Civvy Street. Here, I had a roof over my head, food, skills training and camaraderie with fellow survivors of the Great Depression. It was a deadly serious time, but somehow everyone felt safer by doing their bit for the country.

Most of the people I was introduced to through my national service were working-class or middle-class lads. Some had lived lives worse than mine, while others had experienced a more privileged upbringing. But it didn't matter because the moment I put on my blue serge uniform my past was history. I had a new family and a new purpose because I was part of the RAF.

Many times, my mates who were more educated than me shared their books and their knowledge with me. They encouraged me to write and so I submitted my poems or essays to the air force newspaper. They were published on occasion. Most of the officers I encountered were decent men who tried to help us when we needed assistance or special leave to attend to family tragedies.

Make no mistake, it was a different time, because duty to one's community and country was still a virtue alive in the hearts of most British citizens, regardless of the social set you belonged to. Everyone put the grievances they had against the state behind them for the duration of the war.

The working class had been savaged by the Great Depression and the ideological pursuit of austerity in a time of famine. We had long been accustomed to seeing death on our streets from hunger and disease. We had known the anguished despair of being unemployed for long terms. We had endured the shame of poor relief, brutal means testing, inferior schools, slums and the jibes from national governments who blamed our destitution on our fecklessness. However, when war was declared, it no longer became a question of personal, regional or class survival; it was a matter of national survival. The working class, the middle class and even the upper class were united in this battle against evil. The government, like today's, was a coalition, but unlike now it was a partnership of equals where Conservative and Labour MPs shouldered and understood the burden and consequences of power.

Even I, a lad from the slums, was willing to give Mr Churchill his due and say: 'Cometh the hour, cometh the man.' I even turned a blind eye to his previous demagoguery against the poor during the Great Depression. I knew for the duration of the war he was a bulldog who wasn't going to surrender our democracy to dictators. However, in our present hour of crisis, the leadership stage is empty, as if everyone has gone out to fetch a drink during a theatre's intermission.

VI. Being counted

Since the war and post-war reconstruction, a new political breed has emerged – the corporate lapdogs. They don't resemble the watchdogs and guide dogs of former parliaments but instead sit back, ready to surrender their loyalty to whoever throws them the biggest bone.

With parliamentary scandals that have ranged from expenses to spying, it is no wonder that voter turnout is at an all-time low. In the 2010 General Election only 60 per cent of eligible voters participated. That means 18 million people who were able to vote in that election decided that democracy wasn't worth the bother of a ballot. If the February 2014 by-election in Wythenshawe is any indication of voter apathy then the trend has increased to an alarming degree, because only 28 per cent of voters bothered to cast a ballot. There is no question that cynicism over politics and its institutions is at an all-time high. In a recent poll by the market research company, TNS, only 17 per cent of those questioned believed that elections make political parties listen or take notice of their constituents' concerns.

The malaise against political action through voter participation in elections has become a popular topic with musicians like Morrissey and comedic entertainers like

Russell Brand. Brand, who is widely popular with young people for his stand-up routines and appearances on TV shows, has also taken to writing essays for the newspapers about his philosophy. His view is militant when it comes to non-interference in mainstream politics.

As for the electoral process, the comedian seems to follow Timothy Leary's counter-culture dictum that the young should turn on, tune in and drop out because the game is already rigged. Brand asserts that the best defence against the loss of individual liberty is electoral inertia. 'Why vote?' Brand asks, when the system is just one big bloody joke on the people.

It appears Brand is echoing, or channelling, the disappointment the Occupy movement experienced when their experiment in social change through chaos failed. As honourable as the Occupy movement's aims to highlight and stop the inequities and criminality perpetuated by the financial and corporate sector were, their movement failed to achieve political momentum. But how could it have done? Without singularity of vision, without leadership, without direction, without an answer to what the people must do to end the malaise caused by caustic capitalism, peaceful mass protest will end like all parades – when the music stops, real life resumes.

Brand tried to add credence to his opinion that our system of governance has reached a point of no return when he cited that the million-person march that was held in London did not prevent Tony Blair from leading this country into war with Iraq. There is certainly some truth to Brand's pronouncements that our government no longer takes into account the opinions and the wishes of the average person. He is right when he points out that neither mass street protests, nor spirited debate in the House of Commons prevented Blair's Labour government from leading us into a violent cul-de-sac in Iraq. But however wrong and intractable Tony Blair's policy was on war, we did learn something from it. It was a bloody steep price to pay, but it did teach our leaders some circumspection, because no matter how hard Cameron pressed for war with Syria in 2013, we avoided it.

There have been many instances throughout our history when the votes of British citizens didn't seem to count for much when it came to government policy in both war and peace, but that doesn't mean we should jettison the process completely. Democracy is imperfect, but the principle of 'one person, one vote' is the inviolable building block for any just society. To denigrate it, negate it or argue that it is a waste of time tramples on the memories of all those people in this country who went to prison to demand that every citizen be enfranchised to vote, or who died fighting for the freedom of this country in the Second World War. The system may be bent, the parliament rotten but voting for one's government is our birthright, and it must be considered an essential duty.

Though I understand that he is not from a remotely privileged background, Russell Brand can afford the luxury to not vote because he now lives in the well-maintained world of the rich. However, for the rest of us, if we ignore or abstain from our democratic right to vote, it will catch up to us and there will be consequences to the way we live.

My feeling that voting and making yourself heard is always preferable to abstinence is backed up by the fact that at times in my life the common people *have* made a difference. In my early life I admit there were few victories in the struggle to get better living and working conditions. The General Strike was lost in a particularly cruel, hard way. But the people remembered and thought, 'One day, we'll get it right'. In 1932, thousands protested against austerity measures, the means test and the poverty it produced. It took a decade of economic depression and the end of the Second World War to finally correct the centuries of injustice that British workers, the poor and the lower middle class had endured. But we did correct it.

Throughout those early decades of my boyhood unions fought for the rights of workers, but it was a losing battle against big business. Still, they were optimistic that the tide would turn in their favour. Writers like Orwell documented and published books about the uncivilised way many of our nation's people were forced to live because of austerity. Right-wing newspapers and politicians demonised writers who fought for social justice as communists – but their reporting about British slums, disease and social injustice influenced left-wing politics.

Yet even by the time Edward VIII became our king, albeit briefly, there was no change in the way the establishment viewed the working class, the working poor and the millions who had been left destitute by the economic folly of the rich. That is why for the people of the slums and tenements and the doss houses, one king was as good as the next. When his dad died I, along with other teenagers from the neighbourhood, marched through the mean streets of Halifax and bid our monarch be sent to heaven in a corn beef tin. The royal family was as far removed from our lives as the Tsar of Russia had been from his subjects. However, it became news when our new king went to Wales to inspect the living conditions of his people.

The community he visited had been so devastated by the Great Depression that his handlers were unable to whitewash or explain to him why his subjects were starving and dressed in rags. The King, sickened by the poverty that was strewn like garlands of shame before him, exclaimed: 'Something must be done.' Unfortunately, the King thought that the suffering of his people was somebody else's responsibility. He certainly had the ability to change things either by divesting his wealth to feed his subjects or by urging his ministers to be more compassionate to the poor, the unemployed, the starving. Instead he did nothing but smile and wave for the news cameras.

After hearing the hollow words of the King, the people swore that if the blue bloods and toffs refused to assist them, the common folk would take matters into their own hands. So they organised themselves through their unions, their social clubs and their local councils. Eventually, they demanded that their representatives in parliament show deference to their suffering, or they would find leaders who listened to their calls for economic and social justice.

It took ten years of economic depression and a world war, but eventually the people – not the King, not the House of Lords, not industry – did something to improve the social and economic state of this nation. In the General Election of 1945, the people voted for a Labour party that not only promised Britain a new deal, but delivered it.

I, like most everyone else of my generation, voted for the first time on that day. We voted for the future. We voted for justice; we voted for democracy; we voted for the creation of the welfare state.

Eventide

I. Time

This day is almost at an end. The noise from the street outside my window grows quiet as the light fades. As the sun sets, darkness spreads out across Britain and Europe.

I find our cities forlorn places in the evening because the canopy of night is obscured by steel and glass condo palaces built on the hubris of speculators' credit. From them a sad luminescence is emitted from the glow of millions of flat-screen televisions that burn reality TV programmes, news updates and sitcoms into our collective consciousness. Their light is like the campfires of ancient men, used to ward off the beasts that lurked in the shadows.

As a young lad I used to play beside my mother while she scrubbed the dark coal fire grime from our front stoop. She used a wooden brush with thick, coarse bristles, lathered in hard carbolic soap. To pass the time while she laboured, my mum sang sad laments about life in a rough and ready world. When her day's cleaning was done, and the preparations for our evening tea concluded, she'd say to me: 'Go, lad, and greet thy father.' I'd scurry away from the warm folds of her apron and rush outside our front door. In the distance, I heard a mournful sound envelop our lane. It was the noise made by the boots of workers as they clattered against the cobbles, a defeated army marching home from a day's work in the coal pits.

Today, I hear a similar dirge from the people who are beaten down by our economy. They may make their evening commute by car, bus or tube rather than on foot but their low-wage jobs have condemned them to a fate similar to those who once worked in the mills and mines. They resemble the crofters of bygone days, because our society still favours the mighty over the many. The same sad melodies that my mother once sung to me of the rich getting richer while the poor were getting poorer have again become popular throughout the Western world.

In Asia, political unrest ferments because of both government corruption and a related retraction in economic growth which threatens to impede the democratic aspirations of their emerging middle class. In Eastern Europe, political revolution sparks and sputters on the dry wood of corporate kleptocracy. The Middle East is mired in sectarian and geopolitical conflicts that are without beginning or end. All of it makes me concerned and weary for our collective future.

All of our current problems share one central element with my early days. Wealth and by extension power is held in the hands of too few people. This type of economic inequity shouldn't occur any more; it should only exist in our history books.

In the 1940s, 50s and 60s, we treated poverty and social inequities like we treated polio and other infectious disease: as a threat to mankind's survival. Leaders like America's FDR, Truman and Kennedy, and our own prime ministers, Attlee, Macmillan and Wilson, changed the balance of economic power to favour the middle class. They introduced progressive tax laws that assisted the growth of social programmes and the reduction of poverty. But now governments, whether they are on the right or the left, brand income tax increases as antisocial and a land value tax as bolshevism.

It's unsettling to me that present-day politics repudiate anyone who encourages governments to maintain a civilised state. To negate this fundamental principle of human rights thrusts us closer to the precipice of anarchy. Humanity cannot evolve when its rulers are only interested in the profit and loss of their most affluent constituents and ignore the rest of their citizens.

Still, I don't feel pessimistic or defeated by today's self-serving political governance, or the crass disregard of ethics by big business. Because I have lived through so much history, I know that we can recover from this malady of self-interest, greed and short-sightedness. We humans are a resilient and determined race. We have the capacity to do such wondrous things when we apply our intellectual, financial and spiritual resources to good rather than evil.

However, to return our society and economy to equilibrium will require us to follow the slow and steady march of progress, rather than the discordant dystopian drumbeat of new-age economics. Austerity that is targeted against those who can least afford it condemns our children and their progeny to a world bereft of a social safety net. It ensures that there will be no worker protection and no moral standard of conduct expected from our corporations or our financial leaders.

Now is the hour for action; now is the moment when we must redirect the pursuit of our nation from corporate interests to human endeavours. We can either bear witness to the end of the progressive era, or we can work together and keep social democracy from capsizing into a sea of corporate self-interest. It is our choice to make. It is our decision to determine whether our age will be defined by the 'greed is good' tagline which benefits only the top 1 per cent of our society, or by the virtues of a welfare state that allows everyone a share in the nation's economic growth. We must not let our history be written in the boardrooms of hedge funds and conglomerates, or else we will cease to be a free people.

The current financial tempest has not been caused by a natural recalibration, but by a deliberate attempt to readdress the rights earned by workers and the middle classes since 1945. The chains of ignorance and the fetters of poverty that my ancestors and my generation wore are being refitted to modern citizens. Why is this happening?

In my opinion, it is because the common people's right to a dignified life is no longer protected by law or custom. This country once had a vision and a road map to lead each of us to future prosperity. That map has been replaced with a kind of neo-liberalism that is frog-marching us back to a time that was best left to history. It imperils our survival as a nation, and having been there once before I fear that midnight is about to chime again for our country and Western society.

This emergency is as dire as the economic crisis of 1933 or the military and political threat we faced in 1939. Our survival as a people and nation is at risk, and unless we combat the forces that have monetised our social services and weakened our democratic institutions we will each suffer in our own separate ways. Many of us are suffering already.

Inequality has returned to our country, and instead of being condemned, it is being celebrated in the corridors of both political and financial power. Wall Street and the City think we have forgotten what it was like when our economy and our society were governed by the principles of fair play. Yet there are many, like me, who recall a period when humanity used its most useful social tool – cooperation – to build better communities, rather than to build better stock prices.

We may live in an advanced technological age, but many corporations operate as if we were still in the Jurassic period. In a world of quarterly reports, where a decrease in stock value can affect the dividends of the very wealthy, the mindset for politics and business is kill or be killed. But governments are remiss if they forget that corporations, like carnivores, have at heart only two motivating instincts: to survive and to multiply. There is nothing wrong or reprehensible about revenues, wealth or great income, but when we allow corporations to operate without proper checks and balances, democracy is destabilised because absolute power corrupts absolutely.

For a thousand years our democracy has evolved and been shaped by the enlightenment of our leaders and their detractors. We have moved from a nation that only allowed aristocrats and landowners to have a voice in government to a world where every adult citizen on this island has the right to vote. It is a system that is supposed to guarantee that the broadest spectrum of interests and opinions are debated, analysed and measured before new laws are passed or old customs revised. It is a right we must exercise, or forever go unheard.

I believe that this corporate beast can be tamed and be turned back into a benign creature that benefits mankind rather than threatens its existence. We just have to reform our tax code. We have to return the construction of tax laws and code to the government civil service rather than outsourcing it to giant CPA firms who have developed a tax system that benefits massive conglomerates rather than the general populace.

It is not a coincidence that so many companies remit a paltry amount of tax to the treasury, or simply don't pay any at all. They are allowed to do it because they have lobbied and persuaded governments to make them the exceptions to the rule. When corporations consult and advise governments on how tax should be collected, common sense tells you that they will create a system that is most beneficial to the wealthy and most injurious to the middle and working class.

Similarly, the reason the NHS is in crisis is not because health care has suddenly become more sophisticated and therefore too expensive for the public to afford; it is because tax avoidance is not treated as a serious impediment to the progress of society. Our schools are underfunded not because our government doesn't believe in education; it is because they think that the economic well-being of corporations and the very rich outweighs the social intellectual development of this nation. It is the same reason why universal day-care has never been implemented, despite the fact that it would reduce the burden and stress on working families. To subsidise working families takes money away from the 1 per cent who use their wealth for their own pleasures.

Tax avoidance for wealthy individuals and businesses is a sin that governments condone because lobbyist and corporate insiders have the ear of our parliament, not us.

It has to stop, and a strong anti-lobbyist bill has to be introduced. We have to have a law that bars former politicians, their spouses and their children from working as lobbyists for ten years after they have left Whitehall. To me, it is a simple choice: one can either be a parliamentarian or a courtier, but one can't be both. Society has also got to change its perceptions about virtue and vice. A person or a company that dodges their tax responsibility through legal or illegal means is far worse and more dangerous to the nation than your run-of-the-mill cat burglar.

We have to start treating the grand-scale tax avoidance which firms like Starbucks, Apple and Google have been allowed to perpetuate as a crime against the state. Civilised countries should equate scheming by legal and illegal means to withhold billions from our exchequers with treason. There is very little to differentiate between the moral evil of someone who sells a state secret for cash and someone who stashes hundreds of millions of pounds offshore, preventing hospitals, schools, the military and social welfare from being properly funded.

The harder our daily lives get, the easier it is to subscribe to a dog-eat-dog mentality, where we blame our next-door neighbours for our problems. So it is essential that we learn to see through the media and change our perceptions about who is at fault for this current crisis. It isn't the benefits cheat, the pensioner with the bus pass or the people who have difficulty making ends meet on a zero-hour contract and need to use a food bank that are emptying the coffers of this state. It is the corporations, their well-paid executives, the indolent rich and the citizens of opulence who have brought a decline in the standard of living to the Western world and the people of this country. Had this been the status quo during the Second World War, Britain would have been compelled to capitulate to Nazism because we simply wouldn't have had the tax revenue to continue the war.

During the war people complained about tax too, but the richest individuals still agreed to pay a 99 per cent tax on their incomes. It hurt them financially, but they knew it was temporary, and moreover their contribution to the war effort ensured not only that working-class soldiers had a fighting chance of survival, but that their children had futures as well.

Taxing our most affluent citizens at a fair rate of return to the nation is not only rational; it is a matter of national survival. To do it we shall have to coordinate a new tax system with Europe to prevent corporations from cheating governments of their obligation to the state. We have to reinstate an inheritance tax on our wealthiest citizens along with an extra council tax for the most affluent. I personally support the idea of a Robin Hood tax which puts a surcharge on business bank transactions that exceed a million pounds.

The 2008 banking crisis brought the world to its knees, much like the crash of 1929 did during my childhood. In both instances neither this country nor other leaders in the Western world sought to punish or exact penalties against the corporations, the banks and the individuals that forfeited the prosperity of humanity for the sake of their own wealth and power. Our governments have not properly addressed maleficence in the banking and financial sectors. They have failed to exact punishment for the perpetuators of that catastrophe which ruined millions of lives across the world. The only people who have been punished are the middle class and the poor whose savings were smashed and benefits cut. This failure of leadership, ethics and human decency has upset the delicate balance between capitalism and social well-being.

Let the bankers have their bonuses, but with a caveat that if they are found by the court system to have harmed the economy or manipulated the system they will lose more than their wealth: they will lose their freedom by going to jail, the same way that they would if they stole money from a corner shop.

This national emergency can be solved. But the instruments for recovery have lain unused for so long that people are dismissive of their efficacy. Too often, old remedies are scoffed at by professional naysayers: 'That was then, this is now ...' But just as a house fire is still best controlled by a well-trained and paid fire brigade, so too our economic woes will be best managed by prudent, fair and conscious taxation. As citizens we have to accept that we must be taxed on our income to allow the state to provide the social services that make this nation a civilised place to live. For those who are blessed with extreme wealth we must look at taxing not only income but capital; it hardly seems fair that a few hundred families should be able to retain vast riches for hundreds of years because they influence the politics of the day.

We must use the tools that were implemented to end the suffering of the Great Depression and build a great society once more. We need a true progressive taxation system, which is matched by massive government stimulus on infrastructure. Handing out free money to the banks and markets simply creates financial sector bubbles.

Napoleon once said of Britain that we were a nation of shopkeepers. It was meant as an insult, but it was the greatest compliment to bestow on our people because it revealed our entrepreneurial and individual spirit. However, I fear we are now just a nation of consumers. We shop, we buy and we purchase the accoutrements which define our station in life at impersonal global retail conglomerates.

There is a sterility and a terrifying uniformity to the outlets where we obtain the necessities and superfluities of our lives worldwide. Whether we are in Halifax or Madrid, the interiors to 21st-century shops are as indistinguishable as the financial problems of their customers. The death of the high street is just one symptom of the conformist world we are now living in.

As well as encouraging small, local businesses, we also have to revolutionise our farming industry to support small, productive cooperatives of family-owned ventures over big agriculture. We have to motivate small business to create jobs and prosperity. It is time that instead of looking for big business to keep Britain working, we look to small entrepreneurs who have kept their communities afloat.

II. Survival

I have survived. I don't know why I endured, when others who were stronger and perhaps more worthy of life clocked it. There is no explanation, except, perhaps, that I inherited my mum's indignant spirit to persevere no matter the hardship, no matter the cost. 'Can't just roll over and die, 'cause that's what the toffs expect of you when you're no more use to them.' Or perhaps it was my imagination, my love of books and my sister Alberta's admonition to never settle for second best that kept me going. Or perhaps it was just sheer, blind luck.

When I look back at myself, I see a frail boy who didn't know exactly where he fit in because the society he was born into was brutal and unforgiving. But though it was a harsh world, and a hard time to be a child or an adult, there was still softness in the souls of the people. Even in the slums, people had a quiet grace, which was expressed in their pride at keeping up appearance and trying to keep themselves clean in impossible circumstances.

On washday the women of our street scoured their family's bedding and the few clothes that they owned with a wooden posher. Afterwards, they hung their wet garments and torn blankets out across a back lane. While they laboured, the women, who had known more darkness than light in their lives, exchanged gossip, commiserated on their misfortunes and debated and discussed how to make these streets of ruin more amenable. They were a parliament of wisdom; they eased the pain of their friends who were being abused by their husbands, shared tips on how to stretch their miserable budgets and tried to keep their spirits up by supporting the emotional needs of their neighbours. On the days when sheets beat against the harsh Yorkshire winds like the sails on a clipper ship, those women of my community worked together as one, to make existence bearable and civilised.

For my generation my story is not unique. At the beginning, it was a mad dash for us to stay alive and ahead of the dark tides of poverty and illness. It really was the luck of the draw whether you lived or died back then, in both peace and war. I certainly don't miss those days. I was ashamed and frightened by my poverty. I feared for my future and was angry that the ruling class had deemed my people unworthy of a civilised life.

The happier periods in my life only began when the social welfare state was created. It made my and so many other people's middle years more productive. It was a grand time to be alive and I loved every moment of it.

How couldn't I, when I had come from nothing and now lived the dream? During the 60s and 70s I had a wife who I loved and who loved me, healthy children, a home in a good neighbourhood, a garden to grow flowers in and a job that was interesting and provided me a good standard of living that allowed me to save for old age and make sure my family never went without. It is not that I see those times through rose-tinted glasses, because we had our issues. But we had everything we needed, and we knew that even if we fell down the ladder, we wouldn't fall off it completely.

In my old age I have wanted to recover those embers of fairness that burned in the hearth of our nation and use it to light a new fire in the heart of today's young to remind them that a great society starts with the desire of its people to be free of injustice. Many people today have not experienced the hardships of my youth, but many have also not experienced what it is like to live in a thoughtful, peaceful, community-driven society that was always striving to make life better.

To build a culture that is based upon tolerance, fairness, equality and a decent standard of living for all is not simply a matter of giving governments the legislative tools to generate revenues through taxation. There is more to a great nation than having a good set of books and an eye for finance. It is about shared values, history and a common destiny. Those are the building blocks that form a country's foundation.

We had that once, and it lasted for three decades and

not a half-second more. It was an attitude that was bred during the financial and class upheaval of the Second World War. When I was in the RAF, there was pride in being part of a team that was helping fight the war against Germany. There was respect between officers, NCOs and enlisted men because everyone understood that whether their role in the war effort was large or small, they were contributing to the nation's survival. As long as Hitler lived, it was understood that our existence was tenuous, and dependent upon cooperation and not letting our side down through selfishness. At that time, there was a real sense of camaraderie. Class didn't matter as much as pluck.

London during wartime taught me that grit and a sense of humour are two key ingredients that make a city great. I first encountered our capital at the age of nineteen. I had travelled there from my RAF posting in Wales and it was love at first sight. I wandered around her ordinary streets and gawked at the parliament buildings, the palace, the Thames. To my young eyes, London looked defiant in the midst of war. The air was filled with autumn and brick dust. Sandbags stood like battlements in front of government ministry buildings. The sky was crisp with the smoke from a million chimney pots that circled upwards towards dirigibles that were suspended in the air like trawlers at rest on Whitley Bay.

Later on, I was caught up in an evening air raid which compelled me to take shelter in the subterranean refuge of London's underground. Below ground was an odd mixture of people: servicemen, WAFs, civilians, children. Rich and poor people mingled good-humouredly with each other. Each one of us had our own troubles and sorrows; in the crowd there were war widows, orphans, parents whose sons were in combat. People had bills to pay and their flats or homes had been reduced to rubble by Luftwaffe raids. However, for this moment and every second that the war against Germany continued, we shared a common thread; we were bonded together, like a dedicated family, because our goals were just. We wanted to keep our nation and our people safe from annihilation.

Above, I could hear the thud of explosions and the crash of bricks and beams from bombed buildings. While the raid was going on people cursed those that had made war on us, joked, sang songs and took the piss out of death. When the raid was done, the all-clear claxon was sounded. We emerged from the depths to observe a city blacked out and dark, except where the bombs had exploded and ignited buildings that blazed with an intensity which the priests of my boyhood would have called 'hellfire'.

The next day, and every day that followed in the streets and shops of London, Cardiff, Manchester, Glasgow and every point of land that rested on British soil, people got on with getting on. They treated the war like a bad cold. They endured it because they knew to weaken was to invite the knacker's van to your front door. At that time everyone lived in the crucible of war, but they didn't let it terrify them each and every waking moment. In my experience most everyone wanted to be part of the solution, not the problem. It sounds naïve, but those were times when Britain valued bottle more than class or money.

Today, we don't. Most of us have lost our investment in civilisation. We muddle on and hope that we will not be swallowed up by the financial sinkhole that was created when our banks almost turned the West into a desert of insolvency.

We have become a nation of people whose allegiance is to consumer brands and diversions rather than to concrete values of fair play, respect for the individual and honest work for honest pay. Britain has become a nation whose identity is in transit, though we are not alone in that. Our past courage, ingenuity and heart to face an enemy that was far stronger than us, and to build a different nation, has evaporated like water being dropped on to a burning hob. In our present life, everyone seems to rest comfortable in their discontent. In between games of Angry Birds, people furiously tweet out indignation to real-time news stories about Justin Bieber or Manchester United.

Others still sign countless online petitions that demand an end to child hunger, exploitation, sweatshops, A&E closures, or page 3. Despite good intentions, I think if these aren't followed up with concrete action through demanding one's elected representatives stand for something outside of party mottos, it is as useful as lighting a candle at church for a pound and hoping for a higher power to intervene.

There is no question that many people object to the direction that this country is heading in. Anyone can see it from statistics, pub talk or the general discourse in our newspapers. People are uncertain for the future and dissatisfied with their present. However, call me old-fashioned, but I don't think sharing a story on Facebook about Russell Brand's refusal to vote, or liking an Upworthy article before sitting down to an episode of *The Voice* or *Question Time* should be the sum total of one's engagement with the democratic process.

All of us, me included, have sometimes done too little to help maintain our democracy. We have said to ourselves, I am too busy or not informed enough to be of any help in setting our world right. But we are wrong, and every time we stand aside and let professional politicians tell us what to think and what the problems are we will receive hollow rhetoric from them.

David Cameron once said: 'The test of a good society is how you look after the elderly, the frail, the vulnerable and the poorest in our society.'

But how can our PM know that this makes a good society when throughout his entire life he has mostly only seriously interacted with its wealthiest citizens? If your friends, your associates, your peers and your family all come from the top 10 per cent of a country's wage earners, while your relationship with the other 90 per cent is that you employ them or have them serve your meal at a restaurant, you can't know their pain, their joy or their expectations. Reading surveys or reports from public relations firms about what the electorate wants is no substitute to knowing them through friendships and mutual understanding.

It pains me to say it, but in this day and age it doesn't seem to matter whether our leaders are from the right or the left, because most of them live in a bubble of privilege that protects them from our mundane problems. They don't worry about paying for their kid's football kit, or wonder how they are going to get the time off work to take their elderly mum to chemotherapy. They don't stay awake at night trying to stretch pennies into pounds to keep up with their mortgage or rent payments. Their power and wealth keeps them distant from the sheer struggle for survival that ordinary people face every day in the work world.

Yet it was not so long ago that politicians weren't like royalty or celebrities; they were ordinary people like you and me. Some were in business, others were teachers or tradespeople who saw that they could help their communities better by standing for parliament. Now our politicians stand on the red carpet and talk down to us as if we are incapable of understanding the complexities of governing, but in the past our MPs understood the intricacies of being out of work, a pensioner or a small business owner because they were connected to both the triumphs and tragedies that unfolded in their communities.

Some of our best leaders and MPs have been linked to the people through common experience. Lloyd George and Nye Bevan had experienced extreme poverty, Harold Macmillan had suffered the horrors of war and Churchill knew how to inspire people to do great things even if they came from different walks of life. But today, our politicians are like the last Emperor of China. They live in a city that we are forbidden to enter.

Since the majority of us can never aspire to the lifestyle of our rulers we must insist that future governments really represent us. Salaries for MPs, ministers and the PM should be frozen for ever, except for cost-of-living increases. There have to be term limits for prime ministers, lords and MPs. Government should be as the American constitution aptly states: 'for and by the people'. It is time that we made Westminster less a rite of passage for the elite and truly a house for the public to meet and steer Britain effectively and justly through this century.

If we refuse to engage in the democratic process by not voicing our concerns about the decline of the welfare state and the erosion of personal liberty, we are unwittingly acquiescing to authoritarian governance. Each time we are silent, we encourage those who are more powerful than us or who have a vested interest in the policy of austerity to profit from our silence. If we are tempted to say to ourselves, 'I won't vote, it's not worth it', we have to remember who among our numbers *will* vote, and whose voices will be heard above ours.

Existence is more than a credit score or the sum of our assets. The dilemma is that this economically stratified world which we inhabit – where some are given riches beyond imagination and others just make do – was built over considerable time. It will take resilience and determination to reassemble what we have lost. We have suffered a catastrophic illness, and we will have to learn to walk again. We have to rehabilitate the social welfare state for the 21st century. We have to get engaged through joining either community groups, unions, civic clubs or political parties, and start committing time to shaping this country's future.

We have to demand a methodical change to our democratic system, because it currently is as effective as a 1920s boiler in a 21st-century home. The first thing we should do is make voting easier. This country has to start looking at e-voting as an inducement to increase voter turnout. It stands to reason that if you can do your banking online you most certainly should be able to vote online. We must also coordinate an electronic voting system that will generate more participation in European party elections. We have to look at allowing for online referendums for certain European issues along with council referendums and regional and national plebiscites.

Democracy needs to increase its franchise. It think it is high time that we allow seventeen-year-olds to vote. I don't want people to begin their adult life like I did at the age of seven, but I think by the age of seventeen one has reached a level of maturity that allows them to be electors in both national and municipal elections.

Schools must also do their part to educate young people about the responsibilities of living in a democracy. The history of democracy should be part of the school syllabus. Education facilities should all create model parliaments to show young people how government functions at its best and worst. It is only by educating our young people on politics and their rights that we can build a successful future. We have to free our schools of top-down decision-making and allow students, teachers and parents the right to have a say in how their schools are run. I would also like schools to inspire voter registration through a positive encouragement for democracy and its values. We have to ensure that our education system is more than just a factory to turn out obedient workers.

A good citizen isn't a docile taxpayer; a good citizen is one that questions the role and responsibility of the state in their lives. A good citizen is a person who can dissent against injustice and cooperate to make life better for themselves, their family and their neighbourhood. Political parties, activist groups, charity organisations and the military have all got to go out and engender in our schools and universities that voting is the right thing to do.

Spoiled ballots should also be recorded. If the public is dissatisfied with their choice of candidates they have the right to vote against the selection. Parliament has also got to guarantee that outside of budget legislation, all other bills will be voted on by conscience and not by whip.

Finally, I believe we have to modify our first-past-the-post democracy, because it favours a status quo and causes our political parties to resemble different variants of the same generic cereal. We can transform parliament to work for the people if we introduce a representative system. Such a system would guarantee that seats in government are determined by votes cast, rather than our current method, which locks us into a two-party system. Currently voter dissatisfaction can be directly ascribed to the meagre choices we are given on election day. People are dismayed that whether they vote for the right or the left, they get a government that forgets them the moment the ballots are counted. It is time that elections stop being a contest between the lesser of two evils and returned to a legitimate and sincere debate about how we wish our country to operate. A representative democracy would bring more voices to the table, and ensure politicians are more accountable for their actions.

Everyone, whether they are at the top or the bottom of society, has to begin to feel that they are part of the solution and not part of the problem. The only way that will occur is when everyone in the country puts their shoulders to the wheel to get democracy dislodged from the rut it is currently in. All it takes is the time to become informed about the issues that affect you, the country, Europe and the world. So we have to start reading, talking to people from different walks of life and trying to make decisions based upon a wide variety of information – not just our old standbys.

Change will not just occur spontaneously without our assistance. Life rarely turns out like an episode of *Strictly Come Dancing* – we won't get applause just for buggering on in the face of much adversity. Being engaged and part of a vibrant democracy is one way to ensure that you matter, regardless of where you stand on society's ladder.

III. Dreams

This morning, just before waking, I heard it again in my sleep. It was the sound of harness bells. Through my dream, I followed the noise and stumbled upon an old dray horse that pulled an empty wooden cart. The shabby creature was driven by a man who wore a peaked cap and had a cigarette end resting nonchalantly off his lower lip. I recognised him; he was the rag-and-bone man from my childhood in the slums of Bradford.

I walked towards the man because in my dream I hope that he can lead me home, to my parents' doss. As I approached, he spat out his fag and called out to me: 'What d'you want, boy?'

'A ride,' I meekly responded.

'Not today, lad, I've no time for you. You'll have to make your own way home.'

With that he ordered his horse to walk on.

I awoke with a start and thought how quickly time passes. One moment I was a boy, the next I am an old man. It was over nine decades ago that my journey in this life began. I have witnessed and endured extreme poverty, hunger, child labour, homelessness, the hardships of war and the glories of peace. I have loved and been loved, married, worked, raised a family, bought a house, retired to enjoy the sunset of my years, had grandchildren and buried both my wife and a son. I have been unlucky, and I have been lucky. I have drunk my life to the full, but I know it will soon be over. Life is short. Blink, and it is gone.

So, before we are no more, we should aspire to do something that makes us a better human being. We must become more accountable for our actions at home and at work. In the end the only ambition that matters is that our existence creates more good than harm to our families and our communities. It ensures that our epitaph is written with love rather than regret by those who we encountered in life.

Yet in today's jilted world, how do we teach the young that there is more to life than accumulating wealth without responsibility? It is a cliché, but we must lead by example, and the greatest example we can give is to be engaged in the fabric of our society.

Like all generations, mine was not of one mind. We had different opinions, lifestyles and prejudices, but we were a cohesive and united front when it came to creating a welfare state. Naturally there were different sentiments on how it was to be implemented. People argued about its size and scope, but what brought us together was that everyone generally agreed that it was necessary.

The Great Depression and the perils of being at war created a bond between the people of our nation. We had shared experiences that were profound, heartbreaking and heroic. These common traits allowed us to work together for Britain's better future. Today as a society we are more divided than in my youth. We are split by region, income, race, age, politics and sometimes even culture, which makes it difficult to produce the united front necessary to make radical changes in our country.

There is something noble about a common purpose that is intent on preserving a nation and a way of life. Yet that vision can only survive and be beneficial to all of us if it allows for individuality and freedom of belief, thought and expression. A great society has to gain strength from its diversity. A nation cannot survive if it is just considered a hotel, a place to rest. National identity has to be more than simply cheering a flag at international sports events. It has to be unified through its culture. To my mind, there is no more important way for Britain to define itself and its mission statement than through the preservation of its welfare state.

However, to re-energise our country and gird it for the struggles ahead, we need our young to be committed to the future of their community and their nation, as well as themselves. I strongly feel that mandatory service to the state has got to return to these shores. I am not speaking about the sort of national service that entails square bashing and grinding individuality down to a pulp.

I am not advocating that young people be taught how to be fodder for the wars of the old. Nor am I suggesting that we return to a regimented patriotism that is yellow with prejudice and narrow-mindedness. Instead, we need a national service that obliges all young people during their gap year to travel the country and learn about their neighbouring regions.

Instead of the wealthy swanning off around the world while everyone else stays at home, I'd like to see this gap year become a nation-building year for our young. It is the right time to ask the youth of our country to come of age through a programme of non-military service to one's community and one's country. I don't want them being turned into non-thinking, straight-marching adults, because that is the last type of citizen a social democratic state requires. Rather, I'd like to see a system that takes young people from London to live in Scotland for a year with host families, while their counterparts come to London. It is time that the young travel the length and breadth of this island and learn about its history, its differences, it similarities and its beauty. The people of our nation need to develop an affinity for their country. They need to experience its spirit of equality, openness and diversity. We cannot appreciate the difficulties of being either a Londoner or a rural farm worker in Yorkshire unless we have experienced their lives first-hand.

This national gap year should be about embracing Britain's soul, which is her people. For the sake of our country's future, the young need to interact with different communities, different lifestyles and different religions. They have to learn about the fragility of our environment, about the strengths and weaknesses of our human spirit, and about how we become better people through both setbacks and triumphs in our lives.

Yet we cannot, while we design a new method to enhance the education and spiritual development of our country's young, forget about those who are struggling today. A moratorium has to be instituted on student debt repayment for those who fall below a certain income level. Credit agencies should be instructed to remove from their books student loans that are in default, until we have settled what should be the cost of education.

In concert with Europe, a living minimum wage must be instituted that does not vary by region for the largest economic powers. The living wage in London should be same in Berlin, Paris or Hull. It should encourage citizens to leave our over-crowded capitals and settle in and revitalise smaller communities. Small businesses that may not be able to afford to implement the living wage should opt to make written contracts with their employees that allow for fair profit sharing.

Britain also has to begin to have a dialogue about its commitment to the European Union. It is all too easy for politicians and businesses to claim that Europe is either our burden or our salvation, but people need to have the information to hand to decide which it is. There are too many conflicting reports about the cost of our economic and political relationship with Europe not to have the truth told to us. We must have a commission that hears from experts, lay people and businesses as to the benefits and costs of our relationship with Europe. If our union with the continent is simply a commitment to globalised free trade that exploits labour migration and our nation's social welfare benefits programme to enrich industrial conglomerates, then we have to re-evaluate our obligation to this union. However, if it turns out that partnership with Europe benefits our economy and improves the standard of living for everyone who lives under its umbrella than we must fight to preserve it. I don't claim to have any answers here, but I want to at least make sure I know what the questions are.

When it comes to economic and social democracy, we have entered an ice age. We live beside an advancing glacier of austerity, and no government has an exit strategy to remove us from this brutal lifestyle of diminished social service and rising personal debt. Governments can't or won't fix it, so we have to take matters into our own hands. Ultimately, we ordinary people want the right to a decent, safe and healthy life. We want to be protected from the uncertainties that are produced in a market-driven economy. We want to be able to live in affordable housing and have jobs that pay us a decent salary. We want purpose to our lives and we want our children to have the same opportunities as we had to make a go of it.

It is possible that we can have all of that. However, it will only be realised if we band together like we did during and after the Second World War to defeat social inequality by establishing a social welfare state.

We can solve this, but we have to want to. We have to want it enough to go out and vote in every election whether council, European or national. We have to want it enough to reconnect with our neighbours and make sure that they are doing all right. If they are elderly and need our assistance we have to provide it. If they are young and have encountered bad luck, we have to be empathetic and supportive. We have to ensure that our rights at work are protected. If they are not, we must band together in unions or co-operatives to maintain the hard-won benefits of a regulated work week, health and safety legislation, holiday pay, and right to labour without fear of discrimination or harassment because of one's sex, race or religion.

We have to learn again how to be good citizens and we have to punish politicians who refuse to heed our calls for economic and social justice through the ballot box. We have to stop our social services from being monetised, because their sole purpose was to raise standards in health and education for all our citizens, not to enrich shareholders.

Most importantly, we won't survive as a people, a nation or a civilisation unless we eradicate the corruption that has invaded our corporate world through the advancement of cartels and oligarchies, at the expense of free enterprise. We have to take back control, or soon we won't have a social welfare system, we won't have free or affordable health care, we won't have safe neighbourhoods and we won't have decent schools. We will have the world of my youth, where many people died from poverty and preventable illnesses, and lived short, unfulfilled lives.

My time on this earth is nearly through. I know that death's rag-and-bone man will have me soon. It is only natural that the old must make way for the young. Parents die and their children bury them; it is still a source of anguish to me that once in my life it was the other way round. All I hope is that I've left my patch of the world in better order than I found it.

I don't know if I succeeded but I've tried my best. Thanks to the social welfare state I was able to live long and see my children prosper. I don't have the regrets that my mother had when she was dying.

In my mother's final days, she revealed to me that she didn't think she had been a good parent, because the economic austerity didn't allow her to be sentimental. 'Had to be tough as nails or else we all would have been dead like your sister or your dad,' she confessed to me.

In the last moments of her life, she begged to be forgiven by me: 'I didn't protect thee when thou were a boy from the cruelties of life.'

Before I could reassure her that it was all right, she was gone.

I am lucky I don't have to endure the same regrets as she did at the end of my life. Honestly, I don't know what will happen when I stop breathing. Perhaps there is nothing but darkness and nothingness. Maybe the afterlife is like being an amoeba on a primordial sea, eternally floating, forever without thoughts or feelings. Maybe when I die I will have the opportunity to visit with all those that were part of my life but are no more. If I could I'd like to see my mum and dad in that netherworld. I'd tell them not to fret. 'S'all right,' I'd say. 'You meant no harm; you loved and protected me as best you could when the world was a harsh and difficult place.'

As for me, after all this time and despite my fears for the future, I find that my heart beats strangely content. I have lived a full life, and I have been blessed to live through decades of prosperity as well as hardship. Soon I will hear the sound of hooves approaching and the creak of an old wooden cart that will take me from all of you, but while I am here I will keep doing all I can to fight against inequality and make my little patch of the earth a better place. Right now, however, it is very late, and I am very old, so I shall bid you goodnight, and a brighter tomorrow.

Tara,
Harry

Acknowledgements

The act of writing may be a solitary pursuit, but to produce a book that has merit and relevance requires the wise and insightful counsel of others. It has been my good fortune to have Jamie Coleman from Greene & Heaton as my agent. He took a chance on an unknown and very elderly writer because he believed in my message and my ability to evoke the spirit of my generation. I owe him a debt of gratitude for his professionalism, his guidance and his patience.

It has also been my good fortune to have Icon as my publisher, because they passionately believe in the power of the written word. They are professionals who know their business but have not been made cynical by a hard-edged publishing world. I can't thank the team at Icon enough for their marketing support and their enthusiasm for this project. Without a doubt, I am forever grateful to Kate Hewson, my editor at Icon, for making me a better writer through her patient and thoughtful reviews of each draft of this book. Her professionalism, her kindness and her insights have helped me enormously through each stage of writing *Harry's Last Stand*.

I would be remiss if I did not give thanks to those people who helped initiate this project by encouraging me to submit my essays about the decline of the civilised state to their publications. The New Left Project, under the editorship of Jamie Stern-Weiner, was the first to publish my arguments for the preservation of the welfare state, and they have my thanks for giving me a platform to highlight the dangerous road modern society has started travelling down.

I am forever in debt to Bella Mackie, Natalie Hanman and Katherine Butler, editors at the *Guardian*'s Comment is Free section. They have each been supportive and enthusiastic to publish my essays about austerity Britain. I am also humbled by the multitude of readers who made my essay, 'This year, I will wear the poppy for the last time', a viral sensation.

Finally, I have to thank all those people I have broken bread with in my 91 years of life. You have helped shape my character, my opinions and my belief that even during the darkest hours that mankind has faced and will encounter in the future, there is a beacon of light to lead us through the morass. Hope, decency and empathy are the building blocks for our civilisation, and every human being shares those character traits.

'I have felt the sting of poverty, as well as the sweetness of security and success, and I don't want to see everything we've worked for fall apart.'

Harry Leslie Smith stands up for
social justice, for the welfare state
and for respect.

Now it's your turn.

We all have issues close to our hearts,
so head to **harryslaststand.com**
and let the world know what **YOU**
stand up for.

12384521R00126

Made in the USA
San Bernardino, CA
10 December 2018